THE SURVIVAL GUIDE FOR

Kids with Physical Disabilities & Challenges

THE SURVIVAL GUIDE FOR

Kids with Physical Disabilities & Challenges

Wendy L. Moss, Ph.D.
Susan A. Taddonio, D.P.T.

free spirit
PUBLISHING®

Library of Congress Cataloging-in-Publication Data
Moss, Wendy (Wendy L.)
    The survival guide for kids with physical disabilities and challenges / Wendy L. Moss, Susan A. Taddonio.
        pages cm
Summary: "Provides tools and resources to help children with physical disabilities and challenges cope with social, emotional, and academic difficulties. Helps children stay motivated to make a bright future for themselves"— Provided by publisher.
    ISBN 978-1-63198-033-6 (paperback)
1. Children with disabilities—Juvenile literature. 2. Children with disabilities—Psychology—Juvenile literature. 3. Children with disabilities—Education—Juvenile literature. I. Taddonio, Susan A. II. Title.
    HV903.M67 2015
    613.087—dc23

                                                                2015013112

Reading Level Grade 5; Interest Level Ages 9–14;
Fountas & Pinnell Guided Reading Level V

Edited by Eric Braun
Cover and interior design by Colleen Rollins
Illustrations by Ann Kronheimer

10 9 8 7 6 5 4 3 2 1
Printed in the United States of America
S18860715

Free Spirit Publishing Inc.
217 Fifth Avenue North, Suite 200
Minneapolis, MN 55401-1299
(612) 338-2068
help4kids@freespirit.com
www.freespirit.com

Free Spirit offers competitive pricing.

Contact edsales@freespirit.com for pricing information
on multiple quantity purchases.

To Kenneth Moss, a man who doesn't judge a book by its cover and looks for the silver lining in each cloud. He celebrates the good in others, and I celebrate having him in my life!—W.M.

To Cody, my son, whose empathy, honesty, and sense of humor have impacted so many, and to Alexus, my daughter, who is brilliant and determined, who is the strongest woman, and who will one day change the world!—S.T.

Contents

Introduction

Coping with Your Challenge

- Do you ever feel different and alone?
- Do you ever wonder what other kids with physical disabilities or difficulties feel?
- Do you wonder what they do to overcome problems and obstacles?
- Do you sometimes feel jealous of kids who don't have physical challenges?
- Do you sometimes wish you didn't have to do your therapy exercises?
- Does your physical issue make you feel sad, angry, frustrated, or scared?
- Do you worry about the future?

If you answered yes to any of these questions, this book is for you!

>>>>>> How This Book Can Help You

Since you are reading this book, you probably have a physical disability or challenge. You might have a long-term physical difficulty. Or maybe you have a chronic illness or a serious medical concern. Whatever your condition, you may find that you face challenges other kids don't have to deal with. And we're not just talking about your physical challenges. At times, a physical issue can lead to feeling misunderstood. Some kids become unhappy with how they

see themselves. And some feel like nobody else knows what it's like to be in their shoes.

Of course, nobody can know exactly what it's like to be you. But the truth is, you are not alone. Lots of kids deal with physical issues just like you do. And they face lots of the same questions and problems. You'll meet a bunch of these kids in this book. We have worked with hundreds of young people who have struggled with physical differences or illnesses. That includes kids with physical challenges like cerebral palsy, seizures, spina bifida, rheumatoid arthritis, amputations, and Crohn's disease. Their stories are the heart of this book. We have changed names and combined the details about many individuals, but the struggles and successes are real. Even if you don't see anyone here who has the exact same physical issue as you, you will probably find that you face similar concerns and challenges.

Reading this book may help you feel less alone. It will also give you lots of ideas for feeling more positive and managing your physical issues. It can help you get along better with your family and friends. You'll find ideas for helping others understand you and learn how to help and support you.

"I never talked to anyone else who shared their feelings about having a disability. None of my friends have one. My friends are great and they try to understand me. Still, I wish I had a chance to find out how another kid deals with having a disability and getting through each day."—Alexander, age 11

Kids live in all kinds of families. When you read about *parents* in this book, think of the adult or adults who live with and take care of you. This might be your dad, mom, stepparent, foster parents, guardians, or adult relatives.

〉〉〉〉〉〉 How to Use This Book

It can be really helpful to read this book with your parents and discuss it with them. If you prefer, feel free to read it by yourself. Just be sure to talk about what you read with your mom, dad, or another adult you trust.

You can read this book straight through or skip around. That's up to you. You'll probably get the most benefit if you read all of it. But if there's something you want help with right now, look it up in the index or check out these chapter summaries:

Chapter 1: Who Are You . . . Really? Here, you can look at how you see yourself and who you really are—beyond your medical or physical problem.

Chapter 2: Helping Other Kids Understand You. Discover strategies for teaching kids around you about the total package that is you!

Chapter 3: Working with Your Support Team. Learn about many of the specialists who help kids with physical differences and disabilities. Some of these people are probably part of your support team. You'll find out how you can become an active member in that team. You'll also learn how to be part of the process of selecting specialists for your team.

Chapter 4: Getting and Staying Motivated. This chapter is loaded with tips for getting and staying focused as you work with your support team and set goals. You'll find out how to get started, keep working, and believe in yourself.

Chapter 5: Staying Positive (When You Just Can't Seem to Smile). Do you sometimes struggle with sadness or other negative feelings? Lots of kids do. That includes fears about the future. Chapter 5 has some important tools that can help you.

Chapter 6: Becoming More Independent. This chapter explores ways to take control and create more choices in your life.

Chapter 7: Getting the Most Out of School (And Thinking About Your Future). This chapter can help you start to plan for your next school year, future school years, and even your job choices later on.

In all of the chapters, you'll find quotes from kids and stories about kids. You'll find lots of tips and ideas to try in boxes labeled "Try This." Sections labeled "You Can Say" give you examples of how to talk about things that might seem tricky. Often, we suggest that you write down ideas or make a list of things to remember. You can do this with pen and paper, use a dictation device (like a computer program), or type into a computer—whatever method works best for you. You might want to keep a notebook so all your ideas are together. Then you can refer to them easily.

At the end of the book is a **Note to Parents** that you can show to your mom or dad. You can also read the Note to Parents if you're curious.

⟩⟩⟩⟩⟩ Why We Wrote This Book

We have spent decades working with kids. Many of these kids have physical challenges or other disabilities. A lot of them have told us about feeling misunderstood and different. Many are curious about how other kids deal with a challenge like theirs. We have been honored to be a part of their support teams. We wrote this book so that you can learn from the challenges and successes of others and benefit from our experiences in helping kids.

The main thing we hope you take away from the book is this: **Your physical issues are not who you are.** They are just a part of you. It's true that they can cause struggles in your life, but being creative can help you work around them. This book has lots of ways to help you cope with challenges that you face emotionally, socially, and physically.

We hope the book helps you, and we wish you all the best!

Wendy L. Moss, Ph.D.
Susan A. Taddonio, D.P.T.

Chapter 1

Who Are You... Really?

It seems like a simple question. Who are you? You can answer by giving your name, your age, the color of your hair, and your height. You can answer by explaining your physical difficulties.

But do those things really define YOU?

Every person is a unique individual. It's important to know who you are—inside—so you can focus on your strengths, work on your challenges, and let others know all about your positive qualities. If you focus more on your *abilities* than your disabilities, you're likely to feel better about yourself. You'll be more confident, too, and enjoy life more.

>>>>>> You Are Not Your Disability

Unless you're reading this book to help someone else, you probably have a physical challenge. You may struggle with how your legs or arms work, or with your ability to speak clearly. You might have trouble with your coordination or with controlling body functions (like breathing or toileting). Or maybe you have other difficulties. Even someone who has *all* of these issues would also have many things that make that person special in a positive way. You are much more interesting and complicated than what your body can or can't do.

Check out how Stacey describes herself.

"I'm a tall 10-year-old girl and I walk a little funny. I have a problem called spina bifida. I have to get physical therapy. I wish I could walk better, but I have to keep trying. I sometimes feel my legs get tired." —Stacey, age 10

Does that description tell you anything about Stacey's talents? Her sense of humor? What she does for fun? What else could she talk about that describes who she really is?

Your disability or challenge is a part of what you have to deal with in life—probably a big part. It may cause you frustration, or even some pride in how you overcome it. It's natural to think of it as part of who you are.

Still, it is only one aspect of your identity. You also have your own way of thinking. You have your own personality, sense of humor, choice of friends, and interests. You probably like certain subjects in school more than others. You act in certain ways when around other kids. All of these things make up the real you. No one picks friends just because of how their arms or legs work. They pick friends for much more personal reasons: who they are.

>>>>> Describe Yourself

So, who are you? Here are some words that describe positive traits that many kids have. Do any of them fit you?

funny

caring

honest   friendly   happy

smart   loyal   creative

trustworthy   calm

down-to-earth

optimistic   enthusiastic

reliable

capable   kind   courageous

determined   fun-loving   interesting

respectful   thoughtful

clever   responsible

Other things can help describe you, too, like:

- your interests and hobbies
- the activities you're involved in
- your favorite TV shows and websites
- the music or comedians you listen to
- books and video games you like

A description of you can contain all of these ideas, or some of them, or other ideas.

Even though it's healthy to focus mostly on who you are on the inside, the challenges we all face—like physical disabilities—shape who we are as well. They give us opportunities to learn, grow, and change. How have your physical challenges shaped you? What have you learned from your disability? Have you learned to overcome challenges? Face difficult times? Work hard? Focus on these abilities that you have gained along with your other strengths.

Try This

Write, dictate, or type a few sentences that explain who you are. Think about what you have already learned in this chapter.

- What words describe your personality?
- What do you like to do in and outside of school?
- What have you learned from your disability?

Write as little or as much as you like. If you aren't sure how to get started, ask a trusted adult, such as a parent, to help you.

Once you have written down some ideas about yourself, remember to share this information with others so they understand who you are. For example, you can teach others about who you are by how you act and by telling them about your interests. You might look at your list of ideas before you meet new people. Some kids find that it helps to write a letter to their teachers so that teachers can understand them better.

MALIK

Malik is an 11-year-old boy who just transferred to a new middle school. He wanted his teachers to know that he has cerebral palsy (CP) and can't always walk fast enough to get to class before the bell rings. He also wanted them to know that he tries hard but his hand isn't always strong enough for him to write for long periods of time. His dad reminded him to tell the teachers about his personality and strengths, too.

Malik sent emails to each of his teachers and briefly described himself. Here is what he wrote:

"My name is Malik. I am new to the school and don't know my way around. I know I'll learn how to get around the building, but sometimes it may take me longer to get to your class. I have cerebral palsy (CP) and my legs and arms don't always work the right way. I try hard, though. Really hard. I also like to laugh and I like to have fun. I love the Horrible Histories books because they combine my love of history and humor. Have you read any of those?

"I have a hard time making friends. I think sometimes other kids are scared of me because I wear leg braces, move awkwardly, and don't play sports. Some of them

think I'm weird until they get to know me. Can you help me with this?

"Oh, I almost forgot. I also care about schoolwork. I think I'm pretty smart, and I don't lie. Nothing really scares me, and I've had to deal with some pretty tough stuff, like hospitals and physical therapy. Thanks for reading this."

When Malik sent this email to his teachers, they learned a lot about him, including his willingness to discuss his physical disability, his desire to fit in, and some things about his personality. The teachers got a better idea of how to help Malik. And writing the letter helped Malik learn more about himself.

Writing to your teachers can be helpful even if you have been in their classes or in the school for a while. An easy way to do this is with email, but you can also write notes and leave them in the teachers' mailboxes at school. You can even just set up a time to talk. The more your teachers learn about who you are, the easier it will be for them to understand you.

⟩⟩⟩⟩⟩ Are You Happy with Your View of Yourself?

As you think about how you see yourself, think about how well you like that image. **Are there things you wish you could change?** If so, is it possible to change them? You can change certain things about yourself—like how you treat friends, how you do in school, how you spend your free time, and so on. Other things you can't change, of course. You're stuck with your eyes, ears, and most other physical features, whether you love them or not.

When it comes to your physical challenges, can you change how your body works? Yes and no. Here's an example: You might not be able to change the fact that you are in a wheelchair. However, you might be able to find ways to be less limited by it. For instance, if you have strong arms, maybe you can put a special bag on the side of the wheelchair and take things out of it when you need them. That way you won't have to rely on others to carry your backpack from class to class. This may give you a greater sense of independence.

Working hard at therapy can help change what you can do, too. Chapter 3 talks about people on your support team—your doctor or physical therapist (or even occupational therapist, speech therapist, or pulmonologist). Asking these people questions will help you learn more specific information about what you can physically control and what you can't.

Here's some really important news: **You can even control many of your thoughts and feelings so that you feel better about yourself.**

Maybe you sometimes get down about your physical needs and difficulties. Or you feel it's unfair that you have to stretch or practice exercises when many other kids don't have to work so hard.

If you have strong negative feelings like anger or sadness, try to find ways to focus more on the positive. One thing you might do is think of your exercises as a step toward reaching your goals. Maybe you can exercise with others who have similar issues so it becomes a social time for you. Or turn on your favorite music so you get to enjoy the songs and don't focus as much on the discomfort.

As you do your work, remind yourself that you can feel proud of yourself for trying your best. It can be tough to do all the exercises your therapists recommend, especially if you feel that your friends who don't have physical difficulties could succeed at the exercises easily. Give yourself compliments for rising to these challenges.

Latisha was a 10-year-old girl with muscular dystrophy. Her doctors told her that her condition may get worse over time. They told her that it was hard to know for sure, since every case was different. Her main issue was that her legs felt weak and tight.

Latisha was mad at the world and jealous of everyone who didn't have this problem. She cried a lot and refused to hang out with other kids, even though she had some friends in school. But then she saw a psychologist who reminded her that she had a lot of choices in her life. She could be depressed, stop exercising, and be resentful of others who didn't have muscular dystrophy. Or she could work to feel better.

Latisha, her psychologist, and her mom came up with a plan to help her feel a little better each day. First, her mom helped her make a list of her positive qualities and strengths so she could focus on those things. The list was long and had things like Latisha's sense of humor, her excellent reading and writing skills, and her skill at taking

care of animals. Next, Latisha decided to stop avoiding other kids. She asked the principal if she could occasionally play board games outside at recess. The principal agreed, and Latisha began to take a magnetic Scrabble game to school. Before long, she had a group of friends who wanted to play with her. Soon after that, Latisha began to hang out with kids on weekends, too.

Latisha also continued talking with her psychologist and other therapists to find ways to enjoy herself more. Over time, she began to feel better. "I'm going to fight my muscular dystrophy every step of the way," she told her mom. "Maybe I won't beat it, but I'm going to have fun each day and not give up."

Try This

Here are some tips to help you focus on the positive.

1. Focus on what you **can** do.

2. Spend time with close friends and supportive adults who accept you for you.

3. Keep busy with activities you enjoy.

4. Change negative thoughts into more positive ones, like this:

   - Negative thought: "I hate my body."

   - Positive thought: "Even though I don't like that my right arm is too weak to use much, I've learned ways to do a lot of things I enjoy. And I have good friends who are happy to help me when I need it."

5. Communicate well with your therapists. Share your goals and frustrations. Let them know which exercises hurt a lot or help a lot. Ask their advice on problems you face. They are trained to help.

6. Give yourself rewards for putting in effort!

Sometimes community activities that your classmates are involved in could help you or just be fun for you. For instance, consider joining your library's book club for kids. Or join a swimming program at a local YMCA. Perhaps there's a group for kids who have physical disabilities where, together, everyone can brainstorm ways to cope.

You have a right to wish that your body worked differently. Focusing on the positive doesn't mean ignoring your pain and challenges. It just means feeling better about who you are. If you have a very hard time finding positives to focus on, or your mood makes you unhappy all day long, for many days, then you might be depressed. Talk to an adult you trust right away about getting help. Turn to Chapter 5 to read more about dealing with upsetting feelings, including sadness.

If you want to be happier and keep a positive attitude, try focusing on the things you can change and control. Doing this may also help you build on your strengths and focus on dealing with your challenges. Chapter 4 is all about how to get and stay motivated. Check it out!

Chapter 2

Helping Other Kids Understand You

People often make assumptions about others based on nothing more than appearance. Sometimes kids get judged and labeled as "jocks," "brainiacs," "nerds," "cool," "dorky," and more. We use these labels as quick ways to make guesses about what others might like to do or who they might like to hang out with. We sometimes use labels to judge what kind of personality someone might have.

Have you ever noticed people making assumptions about you? Do kids just see part of who you are? Do they only see your physical issues? Do they label you because of them?

"I really hate when people jump to conclusions. I want them to get to know me so they can really know about my personality, abilities, and struggles."
—Sarah, age 12

Lots of kids don't want to be boxed into a stereotype or have anyone assume what their interests are. If others are guessing who you are, they may make mistakes about how you feel or think. This may lead to you feeling misunderstood and frustrated.

On the other hand, if people *really* understand and accept you, you may find that you're more comfortable around them. You may develop closer friendships. You may even feel more comfortable with yourself. This chapter is all about helping others really get to know you.

JACOB   Eleven-year-old **Jacob** has a classmate named Tara who suffered a spinal cord injury after a car crash. Now Tara can't walk. She can't play most sports, and she even has trouble writing. At first, Jacob stayed away from Tara. He didn't want to say something that might accidentally offend her. For example, if he mentioned his love of skiing, would that make her feel bad? Then one day he ended up sitting next to Tara in the auditorium before an assembly. They started talking. Tara told him that she likes to create funny poems in her head. Jacob laughed when Tara shared some of these poems with him. Now he sometimes sits with her on purpose. She has a funny sense of humor, and in a lot of ways she's just like anybody else.

Once Jacob began speaking with her, Tara taught him that she was a regular kid in an irregular body. Can you do this, too?

Try This

Here are a few tips for helping kids see the real you.

- **Smile.** Let kids know you want them to talk with you.

- **Make eye contact.** This lets others know that you're interested in them. But be careful not to stare!

- **Let adults know who you are.** Sometimes adults can let other kids know about your interests, personality, and hobbies. This can make kids more comfortable approaching you.

- **Occasionally wear a shirt with a slogan** or an event that you care about (like "MTV Video Music Awards"). Other ways to share your interests include putting a sticker on your folder or hanging a picture in your locker.

- **Compliment another kid** on a class presentation or something else.

- **Get involved.** Can you act? Join a play. Do you like science and engineering? Join a Lego league. Do you like photography? Join a photography club.

If you want to do more, you can even ask your teacher to let you teach the kids about who you are. Read more about talking with others about yourself starting on page 27.

⟩⟩⟩⟩ Your Social World

Your *social world* is made up of the people in your life you do things with and talk to on a regular basis. Think about kids you see in your classroom, on your bus, or in group activities outside of school. Maybe you attend a youth group, art class, or swimming club where there are other kids. Do you go to a support group or therapy with kids who share your physical struggles and emotional concerns? These kids are all part of your social world. They're your **peers.**

What do you do in your social world? You might talk with kids at lunch, play at recess, go to movies, play games online, talk about TV shows and YouTube videos, help one another with homework, and many more things. **Are there parts of your social world you'd like to change?** Here are some things that kids with physical challenges have told us they would like to happen in their social world:

- I want to have other kids sit with me at lunch.
- I want another kid to call me at home.
- I want to go to parties.
- I want people to stop staring at me.
- I want people to know that I'm not lazy.
- I want people to know that my brain is fine, even though my body has some problems.

Any of these can be a goal that you work toward. Maybe your goal is simply to get to know others better—and have them get to know *you* better. If so, you can start by talking with kids. Here are a couple of tips to keep in mind:

Show you care. If you know what somebody is interested in, show you care by asking about it. For example, maybe you know someone who likes building robots. Ask about it even if *you* don't want to build robots.

You Can Say

- "I heard you build robots. That sounds really cool! How did you get into that?"
- "I don't know much about building robots. What do you like about it?"

When you show others that you care about their interests, you let them know that you're open to learning more about them.

Start conversations. If kids seem nervous to approach you, you can approach them. Think of something you could talk about, and start the conversation. This makes it easier for other kids. Then they don't have to figure out what to talk about and they don't have to approach you first.

You Can Say

- "Hi! Did you watch the playoff game last night? What a game!"

- "I can't wait for spring break, can you? I'm going to sleep in every day. Do you have plans?"

- "Who's your favorite singer? I love Taylor Swift."

Remember to smile when you talk to other kids so they know that you're enjoying the conversation.

>>>> Your Social Image

In Chapter 1 you had the chance to think about who you are beyond your disability. But your peers don't always see you the same way you see yourself. Your social image is who others think you are (including assumptions they make).

What do you think your social image is? In other words, how do other kids think of you?

ELLA

Ella, a fifth grader, usually minded her own business at school. She sat by herself at lunch and moved around the building in her wheelchair without trying to talk with others. But she always tried to act nice if anyone spoke with her.

One day, Ella found herself at the same table as Annie in the cafeteria. They started talking and found out they both liked the same YouTube comedy series. Later, Ella was surprised to hear that Annie had always thought she was not very friendly. Annie said, "You always stay by yourself and don't really talk to anyone, so I thought you kind of wanted us to keep our distance." This wasn't what Ella wanted at all. She decided to sit next to some kids from her class at lunch the next day and speak up more often in class so she could change the way people thought about her.

Think about whether your social image tells people what you want them to know about you. Do your actions sometimes send a message that does not show who you really are? With a disability, it's easy for this to happen. For example, imagine you had weak bones because of osteogenesis imperfecta, or OI. Your doctor and parents told you not to be in the hallway with lots of kids who might accidentally bump into you. That wouldn't be your fault. Still, it might result in you having to walk to your next class a few minutes before everyone else. You wouldn't be able to socialize in the halls between classes. Kids might think that meant you didn't *want* to socialize.

If your physical challenges are causing others to misunderstand your actions, try speaking with your parents, doctor, and physical therapist. They might have some creative tips for you. For example, someone with OI might be allowed to go to lunch two minutes early. That way the person wouldn't risk being accidentally hurt, but would still be able to spend all of lunchtime with everybody else.

When other kids come into the lunchroom, the student could welcome them to the table.

People with disabilities can have challenges that affect them in other ways—like their mood. Have you ever felt frustrated, annoyed, sad, angry, or jealous because your disability keeps you from doing something you want to do? How you express those feelings can affect your social reputation.

WILLIAM

William, who was 9, had a reputation of "being a baby." He had tantrums in gym when he didn't catch the ball, his team didn't win a game, or he was asked to run laps. Other kids got annoyed whenever he had a tantrum. William had juvenile rheumatoid arthritis (JRA), but none of his classmates knew it. The tantrums happened because he would get pains in his ankles and knees after too much time running around in gym. When he felt the pain, he tried to hide it, but it made him grumpy.

Kids made fun of William for being cranky, and he didn't like it that people thought he was a baby. So he began talking with his doctor and parents about how hard gym was for him. His dad suggested that the gym teacher help find a solution. At first, William didn't want Mr. Montoya to know about his JRA. But then he agreed that this plan was better than being called a baby by the other kids.

Mr. Montoya was glad to learn of William's JRA so that he could help him. He shared a plan that had worked for other kids with JRA in his class. Mr. Montoya always had one activity in gym that didn't involve too much moving (like shooting baskets from the free-throw line or playing a ring-toss game). William could give his teacher a signal when he needed to go to one of these activities. After using this plan for a week, William already felt much more comfortable in gym, and he stopped having tantrums.

Take a minute to really think about it: **Do you know what your social image is?**

Try This

Consider the following questions and tips to better understand your social image.

- If you were another kid, watching you in class, what would you think of yourself? What if you were watching you at recess?

- Look at old videos of yourself. Do you smile? Do you talk much? Do you play?

- Do you hang out more with other people or by yourself?

- Ask a parent, grandparent, or other relative how he or she would describe you. Ask a friend, too.

Once you figure out what other people might think about you, it's time to **decide if you like this social image.** If you do, that's great! Keep paying attention to your social image and make changes if you decide you want to. If you don't like it, how can you change it? Think about the solutions that Ella and William found. You can also try some of the ideas on page 20 about showing kids the real you.

〉〉〉〉〉 Telling Others About Your Disability

Your physical disability may be hidden or obvious. Kids might know there is something different about how your body moves or reacts. They might not know exactly what's going on, though. It's often up to you to decide when information is private and when it's helpful to educate others.

Do you want to share information about your physical challenges with other kids? It can be hard to figure out the right answer for you. Think about your reasons for sharing or not sharing, and speak with a few adults to get their opinions as well.

Kia was 11 years old and had mild muscular dystrophy. She wanted to let some kids know what was going on. During a sleepover at her house with two friends, she said, "There's something I want you to know. I have something called muscular dystrophy. You can't tell by looking at me, and it's not a big deal most of the time. But sometimes it makes me really tired. My body hurts. That's what happened at volleyball the other day. So if you notice that I can't keep playing sometimes, that's probably why."

Kia told her friends that she didn't think it would interfere with anything they all did together. But she asked her friends to understand if she needed to rest more than them. She said, "I'm not giving up on doing stuff, it's just that I need to rest when my body is tired. Otherwise my body will hurt more. I'm not breakable, though, so that's that."

Kia's friend Allie said, "No problem," and Lucy asked Kia to always let them know when she felt tired so they could help her. Kia was relieved that her secret was out, and it felt good to have her friends understand.

There are advantages to telling others about your condition. Obviously, telling kids helps them understand why you act the way you do. Also, kids might think you're brave for handling your challenge so well. They might feel closer to you if they don't feel like you are hiding something. Like Kia, you are likely to feel relief from not having to hide your disability.

But telling is not the right decision for everyone. Is it going to be helpful to let other people know about what you struggle with physically? How can you decide whether to tell?

Try This

Think about the following questions. The answers can help you figure out whether to share information about your physical challenge or disability.

- What would be the worst thing that could happen if you told someone?

- What could be the best thing that could happen?

- Would you like to tell some people but not others? Who would you tell? Why?
- What specific information would you share?
- How and where would you share the information?

If telling others about your physical challenge is not right for you at this time, that's okay. But keep the idea in the back of your mind. It might feel more important to do this later on. If you're ready to share now, read on.

Are you **ready to talk** about your physical issue with peers? If so, that's great! If you feel nervous or uncertain about how to describe your physical difficulty clearly, take your time. Follow these steps so you are prepared to share.

> "I tried wearing long pants to hide my leg braces, but finally I got tired of hiding them. I decided to tell everyone. I just didn't know what to say."
> —Michael, age 9

Step 1: Remind yourself of your strengths (see pages 9–12). Make them part of what you plan to say when talking about your challenges or disability.

Step 2: Think about your audience and what they need to know. Who do you tell? That's up to you. Some kids want just a few close friends and relatives to know, while others want to talk to more people. It's important to pick people who are trustworthy, who aren't likely to gossip, and who may need the information to better understand your behavior.

Step 3: Figure out when to try to reach your audience. One way to do this is to simply wait for a natural opportunity to bring it up.

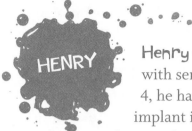

Henry was a 12-year-old who was born with serious hearing loss. When he was 4, he had surgery and received a cochlear implant in his left ear. This allowed his brain to hear more language and sounds. Behind his ear was a magnet that helped him understand the sounds around him. The magnet was easy to see because of his short hair. Henry also had trouble saying a few sounds because he hadn't heard them clearly for many years. He was working hard to improve his speech.

Henry sometimes noticed kids looking at his magnet when they thought he wasn't watching. He didn't know if he should say anything about it. He wasn't embarrassed, but he didn't want to be treated like he was different. One day at lunch one of his friends said her dog had extra-special hearing. Henry thought that was a good opportunity to talk about his own hearing, and he said, "Me, too!"

Everyone seemed surprised to hear him talk about his hearing. Henry explained, "I have technology, like a little computer in my head to help me hear." The other kids asked him a few questions, and Henry felt comfortable answering them. After that, he didn't worry much about telling anyone about his hearing loss and implant.

Like Henry, you can look for an opening in a conversation and start sharing. Listen for topics that could be connected to your physical disability, and make the connection. For instance, if kids are talking about running the mile race in gym, you might say, "I could probably beat you with my wheelchair, but my spina bifida keeps me from running the regular way." This brief comment opens

the conversation, and kids may or may not decide to ask you questions about what it's like to be you. **HINT:** If you are casual as you talk about it, your friends may feel more comfortable.

You might also want to try a more formal approach, especially if you want to talk to a particular group of kids. For instance, maybe you want classmates to understand you better. If so, you could ask your teacher if you can do a class presentation. If you want your softball team to understand you, ask the coach if you can talk for a couple minutes before practice. Many teachers and coaches are glad to help kids speak up. The only way that you will know is to ask. Let your teacher know that you would like to give an overview of your challenges (and abilities!), and that you will keep an upbeat attitude. That way you're more likely to get a chance to share.

Step 4: Make a plan for what you want to say. Think about how to describe your physical difficulty in a kid-friendly way.

Here are some ideas to consider including in your comments:

- when you first noticed symptoms
- the challenges you have with your body
- the kind of exercises you do

- the kinds of tasks that are hard for you
- a bit about your personality and strengths
- things you *can* do (give examples)

Before you end, let the kids know they can ask you questions.

Something else to keep in mind is that what you say might change depending on your audience. For instance, if you are talking to young kids, use simple language. If you are talking to your classmates, you may want to mention that you sometimes need help packing up your backpack. If you're talking to your summer camp friends, you don't need to tell them about your struggles getting to class at school.

Step 5: Get organized. It can help you remember what you want to say if you bring notes to look at while you're talking. If you want, you can even create a presentation with pictures (using something like Google Drive or PowerPoint). This can make it easier for you because the pictures help remind you of what you want to say, and it gives everyone something to look at (so they're not all staring at you). It can also help kids understand what you are trying to explain.

Step 6: Relax and say what you want to say. If you are tense, try breathing in slowly through your nose and out slowly through your mouth. It might help to imagine that you are smelling your favorite food or breathing out in a way that would gently move a feather on the table.

Tensing your muscles and then relaxing them can also work. (Just check with your physical therapist to make sure these exercises are good for you to use.) Start by tensing muscles in your forehead, holding that tension for a few seconds, then relaxing. Next, move to your jaw—tense it, hold it, and relax it. Continue working different muscles down your body, all the way to your toes.

AMY

Amy was a fifth grader and the only one in her class who had cancer. She had surgery during the summer before fifth grade to remove a brain tumor. Now she needed to have chemotherapy to try to stop the cancer from spreading. She would get very tired from the chemo and missed some school days because of it.

Amy noticed that some of the other kids were treating her differently. In fact, she thought they might be afraid to talk to her. Even her good friends seemed uncomfortable around her now. After discussing it with her doctors and parents, Amy asked her teacher if she could talk to the class. She said she would describe what was going on with her physically but also mention that she was still the same Amy they always knew. Amy and her teacher planned when she would speak with her peers. One Friday right before lunch, the teacher called Amy to the front of the class. Here's what she said:

"I know a bunch of you might be thinking I'm sick right now. I'm not sick like in a contagious way. You can't catch it. I have a kind of cancer. This means I have these annoying cells in my body that are trying to make me sick. Right now I'm taking chemo—this nasty medication. My doctor said there's a good chance that my chemo will beat those bad cells, and I'll be fine. But right now, because of the treatment, sometimes I'm really tired. I can get sick easily if you guys have colds or something. So, I can't get you sick, but I need to stay home sometimes so I don't catch anything from you. The chemo also made me lose my hair.

"I'm going to be getting chemo for another couple of months. Then the doctors will check me out. I'm not in pain, just tired. Sometimes I can't do my work because I'm really tired. But I'm still Amy. I mean, I'm still me. I still love the 39 Clues books, and I still love playing Minecraft. I still want to laugh with you guys and be treated like a normal person. That would be the best thing for me. If you have any questions, just ask. Thanks for listening!"

Amy's friends sat next to her at lunch that day. One of them said, "I think you are the bravest person in the world." Another said, "I thought I could catch cancer. I'm glad that's not true, and I can hang out with you and I won't get sick!"

Amy was glad that she did the presentation. She felt proud of herself for teaching the class, and she was relieved that other kids started treating her more like "regular Amy" instead of "sick Amy"!

Remember: You don't have to tell kids about your medical condition or physical issue. But for a lot of kids, being upfront about their strengths and limitations can help them get along better with their peers and feel understood.

>>>>>> When Kids Don't Appreciate You

Most kids want to be included and appreciated. It may be painful when other kids leave you out of activities, ignore you, or tease or bully you. Do any of those things happen to you sometimes? If so, kids might be leaving you out because they aren't sure what you can do and what you can't. They might be afraid of making you feel bad if they invite you to play a sport or game that you can't easily play. It's also possible that their behavior is more mean-spirited, and you're being teased or bullied.

Try This

If you feel like you are being excluded because the other kids don't understand you or your social image is not what you want it to be, ask yourself the following questions.

- **Do you like the kids who are leaving you out?** If you do, you have a good reason to try to change things. If not, it might be fine to just let it go as long as no one is trying to hurt you.

- **Can you tell if they like you or might be interested in you?** For example, maybe they used to be closer to you but something in their behavior has changed recently. If you think they might be interested, this is another good reason to try to change things.

- **Do they know what you can and can't do because of your physical condition?** If there are misunderstandings, it might help to clear them up.

If you like the kids and think that the problem might be a misunderstanding, then you may want to talk with them. See pages 30–36 for guidelines on doing that. If kids are nervous about approaching you, you may be able to help them realize who you are and how to interact with you.

If you're being teased or bullied, that's *not* okay. If someone mistreats you, it's time to speak up. Start by telling the kids who are hurting you that you want them to stop. Be firm, direct, and calm.

You Can Say

- "Don't call me that."
- "Knock it off!"
- "That's not cool—quit it."

Try not to cry or show that you are upset. Your strong reaction can sometimes make people want to target you even more. You may need to talk with an adult who can guide you, especially if you don't feel safe. Adults can show you ways to help end the mean treatment. They can help protect you if necessary.

A good way to feel more included is to get involved in activities that focus on your interests, hobbies, or needs.

When you do that, you naturally end up in groups with kids who have things in common with you. For example, if you like to play the guitar, take lessons with other kids. Maybe you can form a band. If you love animals, join a club that works to protect animals.

You might also want to consider joining a support group for kids who are dealing with disabilities. This can grow your social circle with people who have had similar challenges as you.

Having friends can help you feel cared about, important, and needed, but there is no "right" number of friends. Some kids have lots of friends, and some have only a few close friends. What's important is that you have someone to share experiences with. If you're feeling lonely or left out, try meeting people through some of the ways discussed in this chapter—that's the first step toward getting closer and eventually becoming friends!

⟩⟩⟩⟩⟩⟩ Sibling Frustrations

If you have siblings, or even a cousin or best friend you're very close with, you probably get along a lot of the time—and have disagreements and fights other times. This is true for almost everyone, even those without physical challenges. But a physical issue can sometimes make sibling relationships more complicated. Maybe you can't always do things that your brother does and you feel jealous. Or your sister feels upset because you get more attention from your parents because you need more assistance.

Whether you're struggling with jealousy, teasing, or being excluded, the key to working things out is communication.

If you want your sisters or brothers (or close friends) to understand you, you can try having a talk with them.

Share your thoughts and feelings without placing blame on them. Teach them about what it's like to be you, with your strengths and challenges. You can tell them about what you like to do, such as your love of drawing. Or, perhaps you can show them an exercise you do in therapy and explain it to them: "I'm trying to balance on my left leg. That's no big deal for you, but it is for me."

Remember that a conversation is a two-way discussion. Show that you care by asking about their interests and challenges. Ask them what they want you to know about them.

If you feel left out, talk about what you might be able to do together despite your physical difficulties. Is there a sport you can play together? Perhaps you could make something cool together, like origami room decorations or a funny video. Maybe you could play chess or listen to music. Think about the challenges, ages, abilities, and interests of everyone involved. Then, talk about how you can share and enjoy special activities together.

If anger or frustration have led you to argue with your siblings or be mean to them, you may need to apologize. An apology can go a long way toward fixing hurt feelings.

You Can Say

- "I sometimes get really annoyed by my body and take my anger out on other people—especially you. I'm really sorry. I know it's not fair, and I'm trying to be better about it. I hope you can understand."

If you're apologizing, let your brother or sister know that you will try not to do the hurtful thing again. For example, if you unfairly take out your anger on your sister by yelling at her, promise to try to control your anger in the future. This way, she knows you're trying to be respectful of her. Then she's more likely to be understanding.

If you have tried to communicate with your brother or sister, but you still feel there's tension between you, don't give up! It's worth your time and energy to try to build a close, comfortable connection. Try asking an adult for suggestions on what you can do. Or, you may even want to have an adult that you trust, such as your parent, psychologist, or another supportive person, step in and help you and your sibling communicate more effectively.

>>>>>> When You Can't Participate in a Social Activity

A lot of kids sometimes feel upset or sad when they can't do something they want to do with other kids. Even for kids without disabilities, it can be disappointing when they can't go to a party or hang out with friends. Maybe they have to practice their musical instrument or finish a homework project. So, if you feel that you can't do certain activities, you are not alone.

If you can't participate because of your disability, though, it may be very frustrating.

DAVID

Eleven-year-old **David** really wanted to go to his friend's ice skating party. Kids at school were talking about it constantly—everyone was so excited. But David knew that he couldn't skate. He had cancer a few years ago, and because of that his right leg was amputated. He walked pretty well with his prosthetic leg now, but he wasn't ready to start skating. David got so frustrated and sad that he came home from school and cried on his bed.

His dad came in and comforted him, and after they talked for a while Dad came up with an idea. He suggested that David go to the party anyway and sit at a table by the concession stands. All the kids would be taking breaks, and he could visit with them when they did. That way he'd get to spend time with his friends. David liked his dad's idea. He still wished he could skate, but this was better than staying home.

If your disability sometimes holds you back from doing what you want with other kids, it's okay to feel bad about it. But you can try to find a solution that still allows you to socialize and have fun with your peers.

Try This

Here are a few ideas to consider next time your physical challenge is getting in your way of doing something fun like a party or other event.

- Like David, go to the event even if you can't participate in the physical activity.
- See if your friends need someone to play the music or do other fun stuff at the party.
- Go to the party with a friend so you don't go into the room alone.

- Talk with your therapists about working to gain some skills you can use for those activities later (for example, by adding strength or balance exercises).

- Instead of feeling bad that you can't do a particular thing, focus on the things you are capable of. Host or go to an event with activities that you **can** participate in.

⟩⟩⟩⟩⟩⟩ Having Empathy

When kids or teens have a physical issue, they may spend a lot of time building up strengths and overcoming difficulties. It's natural to focus on your own needs if you have a physical problem. This is not wrong or bad. Focusing on yourself and your goals helps you plan what you need to accomplish and then work to do it.

Your friends and peers may want to hear about your interests, habits, and therapies. They may be interested in how it feels to have a physical disability. But they probably would like some attention focused on them, too. People can feel disrespected or rejected if you never show an interest in them. Ask others about their interests and what they do for fun. Listen to their stories, and compliment them sometimes. Show them that they matter to you.

You Can Say

- "How did your soccer game go?"
- "I liked your report on *Poppy*. I want to read that book now."
- "What did you do this weekend?"

Being social, and especially being friends, is a two-way street. If you pay attention to others, more people may care about you. The larger your social circle, and the larger your support team, the more likely you are to feel included.

If you really want to build relationships, here's an important word you need to know: EMPATHY. Empathy means trying to understand the feelings of others. For example, kids who don't have any problems with the way their bodies work can still listen to you and try to understand how it feels for you to have a struggle. When they do that, they have empathy toward you. You can do the same for them by trying to understand how *they* feel.

Have you ever seen a friend looking tearful, angry, or sad? If you try to listen and imagine how your friend is feeling, then you are showing empathy. Part of being close to someone is truly caring about how the other person feels. So, even when you are working on your own goals, try to remember that friends and family members might need support from you.

When you're trying to fit in, to have fun with other kids, and to help others understand who you are, try to be positive. Look for ways to change things for the better, and you might *feel* better. You'll feel more capable and understood, and you'll have more fun.

Working with
Your Support
Team

All kids need a team of people who help and support them in life. Your support team is made up of the adults and peers in your life who support you and help you make decisions about your health, well-being, and future. They help you make goals and figure out how to reach them.

The most important person on the team is you! You are the one with the needs and goals, and you are the one who will benefit most by following through on the team's recommendations. You are the only one who can really educate the other team members about what has helped you or frustrated you, or what you need more help with. That's because you're the one who is actually experiencing the feelings and the successes and failures. Everyone else can observe you, but they don't know what's happening inside you.

>>>> Team Members

Besides yourself, your support team is made up of many important helpers. Here's how a girl with no physical disabilities used *her* support team.

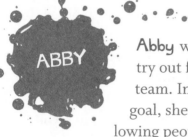

Abby was a 13-year-old who wanted to try out for her middle school's fencing team. In order to help her reach this goal, she received support from the following people:

- Her mom encouraged her and helped her figure out how to pay for some of the equipment.
- Her older sister, who was a good fencer, gave her fencing tips.
- Her best friend cheered her on when she was tired or needed encouragement.
- Her gym teacher gave her tips on how to train.
- Her coach taught her how to fence and helped her prepare for the tryout.

If you have a physical challenge or disability, you may have a larger support team than someone without one. Your team likely includes specialists who can assist and guide you as you work on areas of challenge. In this chapter, you will learn about some of the most common support people. You probably already know about many of these professionals. Others may be new to you. If you think any of them might be able to help you, you will find ideas for expanding your support team later in the chapter.

Parents. This can mean your mom, dad, or any adult you live with who takes care of you. Parents are the people who probably know you best and care about you the most. But that's not the only reason they're so important to your team. Many parents have been trained in ways to help children at home. Your parents may even have helped you do your exercises at times. Parents can also teach you how to speak up to teachers and therapists when you need help. Maybe the most important thing parents provide is emotional support. They are the ones who hug you when you feel different, down, frustrated, or alone.

"It may sound corny, but it helps that my parents are always there to make me smile and remind me that I'm loved."
—Harold, age 13

If you don't feel that your parents are supportive right now, it's a goal to work toward. You may want to tell them what you need—after all, they can't read your mind. If that doesn't work, try talking to other members of your support team. Ask for their suggestions on how you and your parents might communicate better. Page 90 has a list of adults you might turn to for help.

Siblings. Do you fight with your brothers or sisters? Do you think they sometimes are annoying and don't seem to care about helping you? If you answered "yes," you're not alone. But there's more to sisters and brothers than disagreements. Like parents, siblings can provide emotional support and help you with lots of things.

Younger siblings may think it's cool to join you as you do your exercises. They may even feel honored to help and happy to be involved. It feels good to have a younger brother or sister who looks up to you. Invite them to hang out or help you, and they're likely to be some of your most valuable team members.

Older siblings may be able to help you with your exercises and many of your day-to-day challenges. They have been through a lot of the same challenges you'll be going through—even if they don't have a physical problem like you. This makes them a great source of advice and information. They may come up with creative ways to work around your obstacles.

Brothers and sisters will be with you decade after decade, so build up your relationship. Look for common interests you can pursue together. Not only can *they* support *you:* you can be supportive of *them.* Listen to them when they need it, and ask how you can help. Support each other and spend time together, and you'll not only have a sibling—you'll have a friend.

Friends. Friends help you feel connected to others. They can share hobbies and laughter with you. Some friends are not super close to you, but they can still be fun to hang out with. Your close friends may listen to you when you're frustrated by your disability. **They appreciate you for what you can do** and help you when you need it.

Peer support group. A peer support group is a group of kids who all have similar challenges, such as a physical disability. They meet at regular times—maybe once or twice a month. They talk about many topics, like how they stay motivated to do their physical therapy exercises. Group members may talk about their feelings or about goals they have. In a peer support group, you may or may not find good friends. But you will probably find kids who understand your challenges. That's because they've struggled in some of the same ways. They may celebrate your accomplishments because they understand how hard you worked to reach your goals!

Not all communities have peer support groups. Check with your other support team members to see if such a group exists in your town or city.

Teachers. You already know that teachers are available to help you learn reading, writing, math, social studies, and other subjects. However, teachers can also try to change how things work in the classroom so you're more likely to feel comfortable and have success. They usually talk with other members of your support team, such as therapists, to figure out what you need in class. Most teachers are on your side and want to help you succeed—that's why they became teachers.

Special education teachers. These teachers are trained to help kids learn in ways that are best for their learning style. They come up with special education plans. These plans help kids with challenges feel more comfortable in school. If kids need help in a subject, special education teachers make sure they get it. Sometimes these teachers go into classrooms and teach alongside regular classroom teachers. Other times, they take students into another room to fit the work to their needs. Special education teachers look at every child as an individual. They come up with the best plan for each one.

MARTIN

Nine-year-old **Martin** was visually impaired. He couldn't see the flash cards that his regular education teacher was using to teach multiplication facts. Martin's special education teacher read the math problems to him, and Martin told her his answer. He not only learned his multiplication tables this way, but he had fun working with his special education teacher.

Occupational therapists. Occupational therapists, or OTs, help kids build the skills they need for daily life. These are skills you need to take care of yourself and participate in school and other activities. An OT can do testing to see what your skills are like and where you need help. For example, you might have a physical challenge that makes it hard for you to move your eyes to keep track of what you're reading. An OT could work with you to gain that important skill. At home, an OT might help you with skills like brushing your teeth and feeding yourself. At school, an OT might help you work on handwriting and copying notes from the whiteboard.

OTs can also help by providing special accommodations you might need. Examples are a slant board for writing and tests with larger print. It all depends on what your physical challenge is and how it affects your life. Often, OTs work together with special education teachers and regular education teachers. They brainstorm together to come up with the right plan for you at school. An OT's main goal is to help kids be as independent as possible.

Physical therapists. Physical therapists, or PTs, help kids increase their ability to move around in their world. For example, they might help kids move their left or right side in ways that help them skip, climb, or catch balls. The PT also helps kids with stretching and building up muscles. Like OTs, PTs want to help kids become more independent. PTs and OTs are similar, but PTs generally focus more on helping with strength and range of motion. They also focus on large motor skills—big movements you make with your arms, legs, or body.

Speech-language therapists. These specialists often have two different jobs to focus on. Sometimes they help kids learn how to sound out words so that others can understand them. For example, some kids' words may come out mumbled or slurred. That makes it hard for others to understand them easily. For kids like that, a speech therapist can help them speak more clearly.

Other kids don't have problems saying sounds or words. Instead, they struggle with understanding or using language. They might have trouble expressing their ideas in words. Or they may use the wrong words. They might make lots of mistakes with grammar. For these kids, language specialists can help improve their mastery of language so they can, for example, tell stories that are easy to follow.

Psychologists, social workers, and psychiatrists. Psychologists, social workers, and psychiatrists are all sometimes referred to as mental health professionals, counselors, or therapists. They help people focus on their strengths and learn ways to deal with tough times. They are trained to understand feelings. They help kids deal with painful emotions and problem behaviors.

"I wasn't sure I really needed a psychologist on my support team. I wondered how another grown-up could help just by talking to me. It turned out it helped a lot! My psychologist helped me figure out why I was frustrated and taught me some tips for coping with my feelings."
—Isabella, age 10

Psychologists can also help students figure out their learning style and ways they may learn best. A psychiatrist can prescribe medications that can help if a person is always anxious, angry, or sad.

Pediatricians. Pediatricians are doctors who specialize in taking care of kids. Almost all kids have met with a pediatrician at some point. They are the doctors you visit for regular checkups who help your family make sure you're growing up as healthy as possible. They also treat everyday illnesses (like strep throat) and give vaccinations (like the chicken pox vaccine). Pediatricians are usually the ones who figure out which other specialists a child might need.

Neurologists. These doctors focus on the nervous system in our bodies—the brain, spinal cord, and nerves. Someone might see a neurologist for help with headaches, numbness in the legs, seizures, or movement problems.

Orthopedists. Orthopedists are "bone doctors." They see patients who break bones, have bone disorders, and have problems with their joints.

Ophthalmologists. Ophthalmologists are medical doctors who focus on vision, eyes, and disease of the eyes. They can figure out if you need glasses, surgery, or other vision treatments. Many of these doctors can recommend and follow up on care that you need. They may also monitor your vision over time to see if abilities have changed.

Vision therapists. Vision therapists are sort of like physical therapists for the eyes and brain. They look at the tasks a person might struggle with because of a vision problem. Then they help figure out ways for the person to do those tasks if possible. They teach vision activities that can correct certain vision problems or improve visual skills. They may also figure out what accommodations might help students in school, such as large-print books or computer programs.

Ear, nose, and throat doctors. These doctors are sometimes referred to as ENTs. They care for problems in the ears, nose, and throat. An ENT may recommend that you lower the volume on your earbuds, talk rather than whisper, or avoid screaming at basketball games. ENTs sometimes help kids who have sore throats or ear infections that don't go away quickly. They also treat other challenges with hearing, smell, or taste.

Audiologists. These doctors are specialists in hearing. They can figure out if you have normal hearing or if there are certain sounds you can't hear well. They can also recommend treatments.

Teachers of the deaf. Also known as TODs, these teachers specialize in teaching kids who have a lot of trouble hearing or cannot hear sounds at all. They help these students communicate and interact with others. Some kids may learn to use sign language. Some students may learn to read lips. Some may be taught ways to make up for their hearing difficulties by relying more on their eyes or by sitting closer to the teacher.

Pulmonologists. Pulmonologists specialize in studying and treating breathing. Their patients often have lung issues or diseases or have breathing difficulties.

Rheumatologists. These doctors treat patients with issues that affect joints and a variety of other parts of the body. A couple of examples are arthritis and autoimmune problems.

This is a short list of some of the special people who are on support teams. However, there are many more specialists available to support kids and adults. Some of them might be on your team, such as guidance counselors, oncologists, and so forth. The right team for you is made up of people who are trained to help you with your particular challenges.

>>>>>>> Who Is on Your Support Team?

Do you remember reading about Abby at the beginning of this chapter (page 45)? She wanted to have a support team help with her fencing. She did not pick *all* of her friends, relatives, doctors, gym teachers, and others who she could think of to help. She picked the key people who could guide her quickly to reach her goal.

Like Abby, you probably have lots of people who can support you. But you work with certain ones who can help you reach certain goals. Everyone on your team has a special way to help you.

Your support team is not one formal group that meets regularly to talk about your needs. The team may change depending on the time and situation. Sometimes one professional will ask another to join the team. At other times, you may ask others to be part of your team (for example, friends or siblings). There may also come a time when you no longer need one of the specialists on your team. If you met your goals in speech, for example, your speech-language therapist may not see you regularly anymore.

Consider all the people listed in this chapter who work to help you handle your physical challenge. On paper, a computer, or by making a recording, make a list of everyone on your team. Most teams have parents, teachers, and pediatricians. You might consider friends an important part of your team because they help you reach social goals. What specialists do you have on your team? Add them to the list.

RICHARD **Richard** was a 10-year-old with juvenile rheumatoid arthritis (JRA). When he thought about who was on his team, he thought he had the right people. He had his mom and grandpa, his older brother Ben sometimes, and two close friends. He also had his pediatrician, his rheumatologist, his teacher, the school nurse, and his OT. Some days it was hard for Richard to walk, so he asked his rheumatologist whether he should add a PT or an orthopedist to his team.

The rheumatologist was impressed with how mature Richard was being in thinking about his support team. He said, "You really don't need an orthopedist at this time, but I'll keep thinking about it for the future. I like your idea about getting a physical therapy evaluation to see if there are any new exercises that can help you."

A few months later, Richard had an evaluation with his school's PT. This specialist did see some ways that physical therapy might be helpful for Richard. Richard started going to a group in school twice weekly. After that, Richard felt even better about his support team. All his needs were being addressed. He felt especially happy because he knew his rheumatologist would listen to him and seriously consider his opinion.

Now that you have listed who is on your support team, think about how your team is doing. Would it be helpful to make any changes?

Try This

There are lots of ways to improve your team. Think about the following questions to help you figure out if you should make a change.

- Do you have a specialist who knows how to help you manage each of your symptoms? If not, why not? It may be time to think about adding a new member.

- Does your support team share ideas and communicate well? If not, talk to your mom or dad about ways to improve communication.

- Are you making progress? In other words, are your symptoms getting better? If not, let your team know. Ask if they see progress or if they think the plan needs to be adjusted.

If you were born with a physical disability, chances are that your parents and pediatrician set up your support team. Ideally, the team has worked well with you and you have made progress. Now you're at an age where you can have input into who works with you.

One of the main ways to make changes to your team is to add a new specialist.

>>>>> Adding to Your Team

If one or more of your concerns have not been focused on well enough, it might be time to add another specialist to your team. You can make a suggestion to someone on your team, the way Richard did with his doctor (page 56). It might be easier for you to bring it up with a parent first. When you do, tell the adult why you think another specialist is needed. Be open to the response you get. There are lots of reasons why a new specialist may or may not be a good fit. The adults currently on your team need to make the final decision.

If you do add a new specialist to your team, your options might be limited. You might not have many to choose from where you live. You may also be limited by your insurance plan. In those cases, you may have to go with whichever specialist is available to you.

If you have a choice, that's great! Some kids prefer to let their parents choose their support team, and that is fine. If you decide to be involved in picking your team, read on for some tips for choosing the best specialist for you.

Try This

When looking to add a new specialist to your team, the first thing to do is find out what your options are.

- Ask the support team members you already trust to recommend someone.
- Ask other kids who have similar disabilities for recommendations.
- Ask your parents to get a list from your health insurance plan to see who you can go to.

Once you have a list of specialists, try to set up meetings with a few of them so you can get to know what they're like. You can ask them questions like these:

- Why did you decide to become a pulmonologist (or whatever kind of specialist you are speaking with)?
- What's your favorite part of your job?
- What will we do when you are working with me?

You will also want to consider where the specialist is located. You might want to go with someone who is more convenient to get to.

NADIA

Nine-year-old **Nadia** was feeling sad and angry about her physical struggles. She had been in a serious accident when she was five, and she hated that she still couldn't do what she wanted to. She talked about it with her support team. They recommended that she talk about her feelings with a psychologist. At first Nadia didn't like the idea. Was her team saying she had major emotional problems? But after talking about it some more, she agreed to try it. She didn't want to feel so upset all the time.

Nadia was excited that she would get to help pick her psychologist. Her mom shared a list of psychologists she got from her insurance company. Nadia's support team also made some recommendations. Then she met with three of the people. Afterward, she went over her options with her mom. She said, "The first psychologist talked down to me like I was a little kid. The second one seemed really cool. She got what it's like to be my age and she told me that we could work together to figure things out. The third psychologist was good, too, but I liked the second one best."

Nadia's mom also liked the second psychologist, and Nadia started seeing her. After only a few weeks, Nadia already felt less frustrated. And she learned ways to cope with her down moods. She told her mom, "I made a good choice when I picked her!"

Choosing a specialist is a big decision. If you choose a particular PT because you think she or he will joke around with you and won't make you work hard, is this really the best person for you? Probably not. It might be fun, but you might not progress toward your physical therapy goals.

On the other hand, you want to connect with someone. If you don't, it might be hard to work with that person week after week. Don't rule someone out just because you don't totally hit it off, but personality is important.

Communication is also important. A specialist who stays in touch with others on your team can probably help you better than one who doesn't. Your specialist should communicate well with you, too. For example, a person who doesn't listen to your reports of being tired or in pain may not be the right person for you.

>>>>> # Removing Someone from Your Team

What if you feel uncomfortable with a member of your team? Or what if you don't believe the specialist is helping you? Maybe you feel like you have met your goals with a certain therapist and don't need to continue seeing him or her. What do you do if you need to remove someone from your team?

If you feel uncomfortable with one of your team members, try to figure out why. Does the person want to joke around when you are being serious? Does he or she say or do things you don't like? Push you harder than you think you can handle? Could it be possible that the problem is simply that you want to get out of hard work?

Once you have thought about what's bothering you, talk to your parents about your concerns. See if you can figure out a way to make the relationship better. It might be helpful to talk with the rest of your support team, too.

It may be possible to make a change if you and your family decide you really need to. If it's because you have reached all of your goals with the therapist, ask the therapist about whether you can "graduate" from the therapy. If the reason is because of a problem, it's probably best to let a parent handle the change.

If you are happy with your team, there's no need to change it. You can continue to make progress with the team you have. Remember: Even though having a physical disability or difficulty can be a challenge, you don't have to cope with it all by yourself. Your support team is there to help.

Chapter 4

Getting and Staying Motivated

Did you know that the brightest and most talented people are not always the most successful? The fastest runner may not win a marathon. A super smart kid may not get the highest grades, and the best singer may not get a solo in the school concert. It takes special skills to succeed (more on those in a second!). Even if you have a physical challenge, you can still succeed at realistic goals if you have these special skills.

Success generally involves setting a goal and accomplishing it. So success can mean different things to different people. One person may feel that success is standing up without assistance for 10 seconds. Another person may feel that success is learning the social studies material well enough to earn a certain grade on a test. For someone else, success might mean talking with three other students in one day.

Think about what would be a success for you right now. Maybe you set a social goal back in Chapter 2. You might also have physical goals, academic goals, or others.

So what are those special skills that help a person succeed?

initiative

confidence perseverance

motivation

Initiative means the ability to start taking steps to reach your goals. You take control of a task, like homework, without having to be told by others.

Perseverance is the skill of not giving up. If something is hard, or things aren't going your way, you keep on trying.

Confidence means you believe in yourself. You think you are important and capable of accomplishing your goals.

Motivation is the desire to do what you need and want to do. For example, doing your physical therapy exercises may sometimes sound like the worst thing in the world. Sometimes it hurts, it's boring, or it feels like a waste of time. But if you have motivation, you do your exercises anyway.

Motivation is really important because it influences all of the other special skills. If you stay motivated, it may be easier to begin your work (have initiative), keep working (have perseverance), and believe in yourself (have confidence).

This chapter will help you learn tips to get motivated to do your therapies or other exercises or activities.

⟩⟩⟩⟩⟩⟩ Setting Goals

One of the biggest ways to keep yourself motivated is to create goals. For the best effect, make goals that are both

a stretch for you	AND	realistic
(they aren't too easy, and they represent real progress that you care about)		(you can definitely achieve them if you work hard enough)

Both parts of this formula are important. If the goal is too easy, then it may not lead to improved skills. It also may not give you a sense of accomplishment. You may not feel very excited about beating your little brother at chess again or using the proper pencil grip you've used before. On the other hand, if the goal is too hard, you aren't likely to achieve it no matter how hard you work. That doesn't feel good at all.

BECCA Becca had been in a wheelchair since she was very young due to her spina bifida. At the age of 10, she made a goal of playing varsity basketball when she got to tenth grade. She thought this was realistic because she had several years to work hard at physical therapy before she got to high school.

One day after she completed her exercises, Becca's PT sat next to her. She wanted to talk with Becca about her goal. The therapist didn't want to take away hope from Becca, but she knew her physical challenges would keep her from playing varsity basketball. She suggested that Becca make a more realistic goal. When Becca heard that, she got angry and began to cry. She said, "You don't believe in me!"

Later, Becca talked with her parents, doctor, and occupational therapist. They helped her understand that she could set other realistic goals that would feel good to reach. Eventually Becca's sad, angry feelings began to fade. She set a goal of playing high school wheelchair basketball. This would still be quite challenging but also realistic. She worked hard at her physical therapy, remained motivated, and felt proud for working toward a new goal.

>>>>>> Three Steps for Setting Goals

Here's a three-step process for setting goals. Follow the steps to make your own goals and write them on a piece of paper or record them. You will refer to your list of goals later in this chapter.

1. Make a wish list. It's kind of like what you might do before your birthday when you want to let people know what gifts you would love to get. However, this wish list is about gifts you give yourself through hard work. The gifts that go on your list are goals that you want to accomplish that have to do with your physical or social challenges. The goals should make you feel proud and happy to fulfill. Maybe you want to walk to school with friends every day. Maybe you want to play the clarinet in the school band. Maybe you want to make two new friends by the end of the semester. Take a few minutes to create your own wish list. It's okay to include lots of ideas in this step.

2. Circle the goals that are a stretch for you—and are realistic. Remember, a stretch means they represent real progress. Realistic means you can definitely achieve them if you work hard enough. Focus on goals that you can reach in the next few months. It might help to share your wish list with an adult who can help you identify the goals to circle. You can change some or all of your goals to make them less of a stretch or more doable in the next few months.

3. Choose one or more goals to pursue. For some kids, one tough goal might be enough to focus on. Others might want to give themselves three or four goals to work toward. Again, your support team can help you make these decisions.

JARED

Jared, age 11, had a traumatic brain injury. Because of the injury, he was legally blind and had balance and large motor problems. He followed the steps to set realistic but challenging goals for himself. His original wish list looked like this:

- Read a book.
- Ride a bicycle.
- Play with friends on the trampoline.
- Write an essay without someone scribing (or writing) it for me.

Next, Jared looked over his list to see which goals were realistic to reach in the next few months. He realized that all four of his wishes were probably unrealistic in that time frame. To give himself a chance to reach his goals, he crossed out "ride a bicycle" and made changes to the others. Check out his revised list:

- Read one large-text book by myself.
- Sit on a trampoline while my cousin Sam gently bounces me up and down.
- Learn to use a computer program that would allow me to speak my essay into the computer, which would type it for me. Learn to write the name of the essay and my name on the printed copy.

Next, Jared got some help from his support team. His vision teacher helped him get the large-text books. His cousin Sam agreed to bounce with Jared on the trampoline. And his OT set up his dictation program and helped him use it better. He also added a hand-over-hand activity to Jared's exercises so he would learn to write the title and his name.

Once you set your goals, it's time to get started on the path toward reaching them.

>>>>>>> Break Down Your Goals into Reachable Steps

"I started using the ladder for breaking down my PT work into each activity that I needed to finish for that day, and it made it easier for me to focus on each step. Now I even use the ladder for working on projects and studying in school!"—Lindsay, age 13

Even with realistic goals, it may take some time to reach them—especially if they are the kind of goals that will stretch and challenge you.

Choose one of the goals from your list and make a plan for achieving it. Start by breaking it down into smaller steps. Imagine what a ladder looks like. If the top of the ladder is your goal, you want to have an idea of what you will accomplish on each step of the ladder as you climb toward it. Each step brings you a little closer to the top.

Imagine a boy with speech difficulties named Eddie. Eddie has a goal of reading a poem in front of his class. He has trouble pronouncing certain sounds, and he often speaks too quickly. Sometimes he forgets to breathe. He needs to overcome each of those difficulties in order to reach his goal.

Here's what Eddie's ladder might look like:

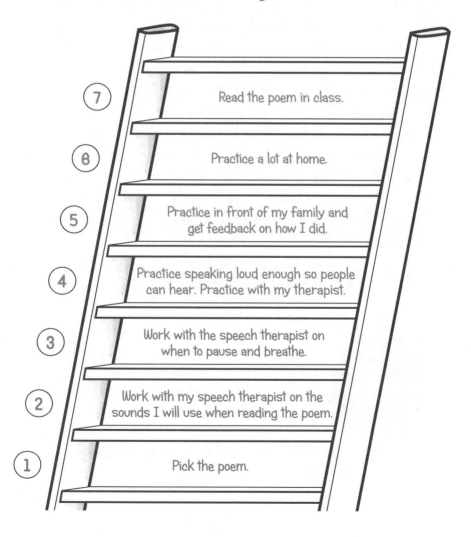

7 — Read the poem in class.

6 — Practice a lot at home.

5 — Practice in front of my family and get feedback on how I did.

4 — Practice speaking loud enough so people can hear. Practice with my therapist.

3 — Work with the speech therapist on when to pause and breathe.

2 — Work with my speech therapist on the sounds I will use when reading the poem.

1 — Pick the poem.

Try This

Choose one of your realistic goals to break down into steps. Then think about the things you need to know and be able to do. Think about the reasons why the goal is a challenge for you. All those reasons are areas to work on, so each one might be a step for you to take. **Each step should bring you closer to the top of the ladder.** Your therapists, doctors, teachers, and even parents can be helpful in creating this plan. You don't have to do it entirely on your own.

You can record your goal and the step-by-step plan by writing it down, typing it, or talking into a machine that records your voice. You can also make a copy of the ladder worksheet on page 80 or download and print it out at www.freespirit.com/survival-guide and use that. There is no magic number of steps. Fill in as many as you need. The number of steps to your goal depends on the number of things you need to do to reach it. Save your plan someplace where you can refer to it as you move through each step toward your ultimate goal.

ALEXA

Alexa was a 10-year-old with cerebral palsy (CP). Her goal was to get on and off the bus with her backpack by herself. Here are the steps that Alexa and her physical therapist created to help her reach her goal:

1. While wearing her backpack, practice stepping up and down blocks and steps at physical therapy.

2. Work with weights to increase her arm strength. This would help her support herself by using the handrail on the bus as she walks up the stairs.

3. Increase her speed going up and down the steps while wearing her backpack.

4. Do balance activities so her balance improves for walking on the stairs.

5. With her PT, practice using the stairs on the bus while it isn't being used by anyone else.

6. The top of the ladder: Go onto the bus with her backpack on.

Once she took the time to break down her goal, Alexa knew her game plan. When she worked on each step, it was easier to stay motivated than she thought. She kept thinking about the goal and how good she would feel when she did it.

When you can see yourself moving closer and closer to your goals, it's easier to stay motivated. However, setbacks can happen.

If you hit setbacks, it's natural to feel discouraged and want to take a break. If you do take a break, make sure it's not a long one. You don't want to lose the skills you already attained. And you do not want to lose time before working to move past the setback.

"After I went through a growth spurt, my muscles were a lot tighter and I had to spend so much more time stretching. I was so frustrated and angry, I stopped doing any of my exercises."
—Marco, age 12

>>>>>> Four Other Ways to Get (and Stay!) Motivated

> "I hated doing wall squats in therapy. My PT wanted me to do 20 squats a day. Ugh! But then I started doing them while I watched my favorite TV show and the time passed faster."
> —Scott, age 11

Setting goals and making a plan for reaching them is a great way to motivate yourself. But there are other things you can do.

1. Know what makes you tick. If you know what you like, it's easier to follow through on the hard work that leads to accomplishing goals.

For example, therapies can be difficult or even annoying at times. How can you stay motivated when you just don't want to do the work? Sometimes you can negotiate with your support team on the *way* you do the exercises.

Try This

Here are some things you might be able to negotiate with your therapist. Would any of these changes make you more motivated?

- Can you listen to music while doing exercises?
- Can you make an exercise into a game (like moving through an obstacle course)?
- Can you choose the time that is more comfortable for you to do the work?

- Can you choose the place to do the therapy (for example, in the gym before school)?
- Can you talk with your speech therapist about your fun weekend activities while you try to work on speaking clearly?
- Can you do a project for class while working on your handwriting in occupational therapy?

2. Build up strengths, not just weaknesses. If you have been struggling with an illness or a physical problem for a long time, you probably have focused a lot on overcoming your difficulty. This certainly makes sense, so keep up the good work!

However, it's also important to build up your strengths. If you love baking with your dad, try learning new recipes. If you're good at swimming, work to be an even better swimmer. If you enjoy socializing, make time to hang out with other people to keep your social skills strong. Focusing on areas that come more easily to you can help you feel more confident and upbeat. That makes it easier to stay motivated in areas that are more of a challenge.

What are your strengths? If you're not sure, check out the following words and phrases and see if any of them might be a strength for you. This is not a complete list by any means. It's just a way to get your ideas flowing.

drawing
swimming dancing
baking
spelling
writing
sense of humor being kind science music
cooking
math singing painting debating
taking care of animals working with computers being thoughtful sewing
reading
video games soccer skiing organizing
other sports fashion being outgoing
honesty

Another way to think about your strengths is to consider what you love to do or are good at. What do you do as a hobby when you have free time? If you still aren't sure about your talents or strengths, ask your support team. Many adults are good at seeing the strengths in other people. It might even be fun to hear from them what they think you're great at!

3. Reward yourself. Even adults are motivated by rewards. Maybe they are motivated to work extra hard to get a better job. Or perhaps they put hours into building a bookcase for their child's birthday, and their reward is the big smile they get in return.

The two main types of rewards for adults and kids are *extrinsic* and *intrinsic*.

Extrinsic rewards are what most people talk about when they talk about rewards. These are gifts that other people give you (or you give yourself). Think of trophies, toys, video games, money, going to the "treasure chest" or "prize box" in occupational therapy, and other treats. Extrinsic rewards also include activities that you might be able to do. Maybe you get extra TV time one night or you have a friend sleep over after reaching a goal.

> "My aunt said something really important to me last year. She said that she knows how hard I try to get my legs to be stronger, but I need time to just have fun and do things I like, too. I started drawing, and my dad signed me up for a drawing class. I make sure to draw every week so I can watch my skills get better and better. It makes me feel good and normal!"
> —Robert, age 12

Here are some examples of extrinsic rewards. Would any of these help motivate you? If your extrinsic rewards require buying something, you will probably need to get a parent's approval first.

- Put stickers on a sticker chart as you work toward a prize.
- Get a toy, game, or video game.
- Get a book or movie you want.
- Have a sleepover.
- Have a slightly later bedtime for one or more nights.
- Go out to lunch on the weekend with a grandparent.

Intrinsic rewards come from inside you. They are rewards you give yourself with words or good feelings. Intrinsic rewards are invisible but very powerful. Have you ever done something that made you feel proud of yourself? Working hard and not giving up can lead to this kind of pride. Helping another child, with or without a disability, can also lead to an intrinsic reward that's better than any trophy or gift. ("I made a difference in someone else's life! Yeah!")

What kind of intrinsic rewards do you give yourself when you master each step toward your goal?

Compliment yourself.
("I rock! I set a goal and never gave up.")

Gain confidence.
("Since I reached one goal, I can reach another!")

Feel proud.
("I feel great that I worked so hard.")

List a few extrinsic and intrinsic rewards that would motivate you. Remember, if your extrinsic rewards involve buying things, be sure to check with a parent or other adult to get their okay. It's important to make sure your rewards are effective and realistic. In other words, they will be effective in motivating you, and they are possible to get.

Once you know that all your rewards are realistic and effective in motivating you, put them on a paper and have that list visible in your room. While seeing an improvement in your physical skills is an amazing reward, you may still feel annoyed, tired, or sad about all the work you need to do. Sometimes, looking at your reward list can help keep you motivated.

4. Use team motivation. Have you ever watched sports players giving each other high fives or body bumps as they celebrate victories? It can be really fun to be a member of a team.

If that sounds good to you, you can ask your therapists if they know of other kids who are working to improve their bodies in similar ways to you. If they do, find out if it's possible to meet or work out with them. You will probably still have individual goals that require you to work one-on-one with therapists sometimes. But group work might be an option for you at other times. For some kids, that can be more motivating than working alone.

Charlie was a 9-year-old boy who was born with muscular dystrophy. For most of his life, he got one therapy or another. He always worked alone with his therapists. Charlie enjoyed talking with the adults because they were nice and knew a lot about his muscular dystrophy. But he felt really different because he never got to work out with other kids with physical challenges.

One day, he was in a bad mood at home. His mother asked him what was bothering him. Charlie told her about feeling different from everybody else. He asked his mother if he could meet another kid with his problems. Later that week, Charlie's mother spoke with his therapy team and found out that there was a physical therapy group on Saturday mornings at a local clinic.

Charlie joined the group. He was shy at first, but slowly got to know some of the other kids. It was great for Charlie to hear them talk about how they felt because of their physical difficulties. Even better was hearing how they had overcome some obstacles. Charlie felt understood by these other kids. He liked them, he felt like he fit in, and he enjoyed being part of this group.

What about you? Would working in a group and getting to know kids who struggle with physical issues help you feel less different and more motivated? If so, speak up!

The most important thing to remember about keeping yourself motivated is that motivation comes from inside you. This is true even when you're working with others in a group. Your support team is there to help you, and many other kids have been through similar struggles as you. But the hard work of following through on what you need to do is done by one person—**YOU**. You can do it!

Goal Ladder

- Photocopy or print this page from www.freespirit.com/survival-guide. Write your goal on the top rung of the ladder.

- On a separate sheet of paper, note the steps you need to take to reach your goal. Then write those steps on this form, from the bottom up, leading to your goal.

- Number the steps from the bottom up.

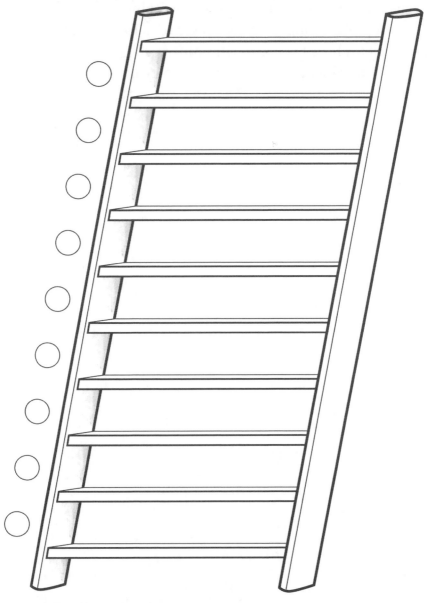

Staying Positive
(When You Just Can't Seem to Smile)

Y ou probably know that even kids without physical problems sometimes feel discouraged, angry, sad, or afraid. All people have feelings, and it's natural to have unpleasant ones now and then.

But kids with physical difficulties may sometimes have particularly painful emotions. They may feel upset when they struggle to do things that come more easily to other

81

kids. Do you feel angry that you have more physical challenges than other kids? Do you sometimes focus on your disability and get annoyed, sad, or overwhelmed by it? Do you have fears about your future?

It's okay to have all of these feelings—feelings are normal. However, if negative emotions take up a lot of your time and energy, you may find it harder to enjoy good times. You might struggle to accomplish things, and you might have trouble connecting with others.

CARLY

Carly was an eighth grader with cerebral palsy. She often felt annoyed when other kids complained about their problems. When Andrew got upset because he didn't make the traveling baseball team, Carly told him he was spoiled. When Nina was sad and embarrassed because she scored low in her singing competition, Carly snapped at her. "Big deal," she said. "At least you can walk and play in P.E. with everyone else." Then she rolled her wheelchair away as fast as she could.

Do you agree with how Carly responded to the other kids? If there are no wrong feelings, are Andrew and Nina allowed to feel bad about their struggles?

It's okay to admit that some things seem harder for you than they do for other kids. But building up anger and resentment, like Carly did, can keep you from making friends. It can keep you from understanding how others feel. Even worse, it can prevent you from focusing on yourself and feeling better.

Comparing yourself to others is a great way to become disappointed, upset, or too competitive. Comparing yourself to YOURSELF is what's important. That means tracking your progress toward achieving your realistic goals and feeling excited when you notice improvement.

This chapter has specific tips and tools for focusing on yourself and feeling better about your abilities—and even your disability. That way you can find ways to focus on the good things in your life!

Need Help Now?

If you are feeling really sad or upset right now, talk to a trusted adult right away. Page 90 has a list of adults who might be able to help you talk about your feelings. If one person is too busy or not available, ask another. Keep trying until you find someone to help.

If you feel alone and you can't find anyone to help you, what can you do? You can write or dictate (with a computer program) your thoughts in your journal, use positive self-talk (see page 84), or focus on something that might put a smile on your face. If you feel overwhelmed and are thinking of hurting yourself, call 911 immediately. People there answer the phones all day and all night. They are trained to connect you with the right people to help you.

»»»» Use Positive Self-Talk

It may be hard to believe, but what you think can change how you feel. If you insult yourself and focus on what you can't do, you may feel helpless or sad. But if you compliment yourself or focus on progress, you may feel more optimistic.

Of course you want to be realistic about your strengths and weaknesses. It doesn't help to pretend you have abilities you don't. But you can always be kind to yourself. **Everyone has strengths. Focus on them!** Treat yourself as well as you would treat a good friend. Compliment yourself for working hard, not giving up, and finding ways to work around your disability.

What are your strengths? What progress have you made that you can feel good about? Make a list of everything you can think of. If it helps, go back to pages 9–12 in Chapter 1 and review the positive self-image you came up with for yourself. Your support team can help you come up with ideas, too.

You Can Say

- "I'm a good friend."
- "Reading is tough for me, but I rock at math."
- "I work hard at my exercises, and I'm making progress."
- "I read the news a lot, and I know a lot more about world politics than most kids my age."

It can be hard to stay positive. Sometimes people get a negative idea in their head, and they can't stop thinking about it. When they have these negative thoughts, it can be harder to put in the effort to improve. That can lead you to feeling even more sad and defeated.

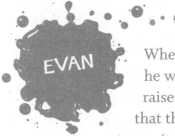

When **Evan** was 8 years old, he believed he would never use his right arm or even raise it in the air. His doctor told him that through hard work he *would* be able to use it—but Evan was sure she was wrong. He got mad at his PT for making him do exercises to help the arm because he thought it was pointless. He felt helpless and sad.

But Evan's PT talked with him about staying positive. As Evan got older, he began to see progress in how much he could use his arm. As he saw progress, it was easier to feel more positive. And as he felt more positive, it was easier to keep working. It took a lot of hard work, but by the time he was 11 he was raising his hand in class to ask a question.

What kind of talk do you have in your head? Do you say positive things like "I can try" or negative things like "I will never get better" and "I can never be happy in this body"?

You can practice saying positive things to yourself in your mind in order to feel better. Saying these good things to yourself is called positive self-talk.

Try This

Positive self-talk is deliberately saying encouraging things to yourself in your mind so you feel better about yourself. Here are some guidelines.

- Compliment yourself on specific progress you have made.
- Remind yourself of your strengths (see Chapter 1).
- Focus on your abilities.
- Make your compliments realistic (don't tell yourself you're the fastest kid in school if it's not really true).
- Remind yourself of goals you've achieved.
- Never insult yourself.

Positive self-talk is about making choices about what to focus on. If you hear negative self-talk in your head, try to turn the thought around. For example, maybe you think, "It stinks that I can't play dodgeball with those kids because I'm in a wheelchair." Change the focus of your thought. It's okay to acknowledge the part that stinks—hey, it does stink if you want to play and can't. But don't make that the main part of your thought. Shift your focus to something else: "I can't play dodgeball, but I can catch and throw a beach ball. I have friends who love to play catch with me."

It's important to learn to accept the things that you don't have control over. That way you don't get frustrated trying to change them. You may be surprised at how much better you can feel if you accept what you can't change and figure out what you can change. Then work to change those things that you can.

It's not always easy to accept what you can't change.

Imagine if you wanted to walk onto the stage to get your diploma after graduating from middle school. If that won't be possible because of your physical condition, it won't help you to keep thinking about it. Instead, focus on how you can participate in the ceremony. Think about how you feel about graduating. Think about what you have accomplished to get there. If you can do that, you're likely to feel pride instead of frustration.

What are some of the negative thoughts that get you down? Make a list of them, and then make a list of ways to turn each one into a more positive thought. Focus on who you are! Here are some examples of how to turn a negative thought around.

Negative Thought	Turn It Around!
I hate that my hearing disability makes it so hard to talk with kids in the lunchroom. I feel totally left out.	It's hard to socialize at lunch, but I have fun hanging out with kids at home and at recess. People think I'm pretty funny, and they want to be with me.
It's so embarrassing that I have to leave class early to make it to the next class on time!	I have to leave early, but my friends are really cool about making sure I don't miss anything important. It feels good that they want to help me.
I wish I could just run around like everyone else. It's not fair.	I can't play like that, but I have lots of fun in other ways.
A kid at school makes fun of the way I walk. I hate that.	I don't want to be friends with that kid anyway. I'm lucky—I have a best friend, and my family loves me. I can tune out that one kid's words or tell the principal if it gets bad.

⟩⟩⟩⟩⟩ Talk About Feelings with a Trusted Adult

Sometimes you might feel depressed or sad because of your physical difficulties. Or you might be jealous or angry at others who don't have them. No matter what your feelings are, they are normal. But if you act out on your feelings (for example, by punching or bullying someone), or if negative feelings are making it hard to enjoy life, then you might need help coping with them. One way is to talk to an adult you trust.

It's not always easy to talk about feelings. It can be hard to find the right words to describe them, and sometimes it can feel embarrassing. But if you find someone who can understand and accept you and your feelings, talking can be a relief. You may feel less alone once you know that someone understands how you feel. You might feel like you have a teammate or partner who can help you handle the feelings. Sometimes a hug from a parent after you share your feelings can help. Knowing that a friend is there to encourage and support you can help, too!

If you read Chapter 2, you learned steps for telling people about your physical condition (see pages 27–36). The steps for talking about your feelings are similar.

⟩⟩⟩⟩⟩ Six Steps for Talking About Feelings

Step 1: Remind yourself of your strengths (see pages 9–12). Make them part of what you plan to say when talking about your feelings.

Step 2: Think about who you want to talk to. Who do you trust to listen to you? Some possibilities might include:

aunt dad mom grandparent

brother

close family friend uncle sister

school counselor

teacher

occupational therapist physical therapist

speech therapist

psychologist

Step 3: Figure out when would be a good time to talk. For example, if you're going to talk with your dad, make sure he isn't busy getting your little brother ready for school or working on the computer. You want to make sure the person can focus on what you're saying and won't be distracted. If you want to talk with someone outside your family, you might make a plan to meet somewhere. If you decide to talk with your doctor or someone else on your support team, you can bring it up during an appointment.

Step 4: Make a plan for what you want to say. A lot of kids have trouble with this step. Since no one is living in your body but you, you are the expert on what it feels like. Maybe you want to talk about how it feels to be living your life in your body. Maybe you simply want to describe emotions that you experience a lot, like *sad, mad, confused, frustrated,* or *jealous.* Then you can add why you feel these emotions.

You Can Say

- "Dad, can I talk to you about something? Sometimes I get so mad at kids at school who leave me out of everything. They think I'm no fun just because I'm in a wheelchair."

- "I'm so sad these days. Sometimes I just think, *Why me?*"

- "Seeing everyone running around having fun at recess makes me so jealous. Then I get mad at them, like they're purposely having fun without me. I know it's not fair, but I can't help it."

Step 5: Get organized. If you think you might need reminders of what you want to say, make a list or some notes and bring them with you.

Step 6: Relax and say what you want to say. If you're nervous, try one of the relaxation exercises on page 33.

JAYDEN

Jayden was an 11-year-old boy with a seizure disorder. After reading about seizures online, he started to get very worried and upset about his future. One Saturday each month, he and his Uncle Ted got together for breakfast. Jayden decided to talk about his feelings with his uncle. He knew that his uncle understood what his seizure disorder was all about. Uncle Ted was always on his side.

Jayden took a deep breath and told his uncle about what he had read online. "I'm really upset," he said. "I'm scared. It said I can't drive a car when I'm older if my seizures don't stop. I'm going to be different from everyone else. I won't even be able to leave my parents because I will need them to drive me around. I'm going to be 40 and staying with 'Mommy' and 'Daddy.' How embarrassing!"

Jayden started crying. His uncle listened to him, and he admitted that he didn't know how independent Jayden would be. Of course Jayden would rather have heard his uncle tell him that he would definitely get to live an independent life. But he appreciated that Uncle Ted told him the truth. Jayden was surprised to realize that he felt a little better after talking and crying, even though he didn't get the answer he wanted. He felt relieved to have expressed his worries.

Jayden and his uncle later told Jayden's parents about his fears. Jayden also shared them with his neurologist. He learned of ways that adults can be independent even if they can't drive. He also learned that there is some real hope that his seizures will be controlled by the time he's old enough to drive. Jayden used positive self-talk. He said to himself, "I will be independent whether my seizures stop or not. I can keep working on being responsible and independent." After talking with these adults on his support team, he felt more in control of his life.

Talking about your feelings is not only a good way to feel better. It's also a good way to get ideas and help. The more people you talk to, the more people can brainstorm ways to help you deal with your painful feelings. In addition, those people may be able to remind you about your strengths or remind you of progress you've made toward goals. These reminders may help you focus a bit more on your accomplishments!

>>>>> Coping with Your Fears

Almost everyone has at least one thing they feel worried or afraid about. Some people hide their fears so it seems like they don't have any. Others may be open about their concerns. Fears may prevent you from enjoying opportunities, people, or adventures, so it's important to figure out how to work through them. Knowing

"I don't care if other kids think I'm weird. I hate sleepovers because I still miss my parents. I know I'll get over it one day, but right now sleepovers still make me nervous and I tell kids about that if they invite me to one."—Gloria, age 10

what you fear or what creates anxiety for you can be the first step toward dealing with it.

Imagine that you are reading a book when you realize the building is on fire. Would you stay put until you finish your book? No! Most people would fear the fire and run out of the building or scream for help. Fear can help you react quickly.

Fear can also *motivate* us. Maybe fear motivates you to study because you worry about getting bad grades. Or it motivates you to practice the flute because you worry about embarrassing yourself when you play in a concert. So fear can have value sometimes. Fear of danger can keep us safe. Fear of failure can drive us to prepare, practice, and do better.

Other times fear can hold us back. Maybe you would really love being in a play at your school, but you're afraid of being laughed at. What if you're so afraid that you never try out for the play? Your fear is keeping you from doing something that would make you happy. What if you're afraid that you will never use your legs again, so you give up on your exercises because you don't want to try and fail?

Sometimes it's hard to tell if a fear is keeping you safe or holding you back.

GRACE

Grace's disability made it hard for her to keep her balance. The summer after sixth grade, she really wanted to try inline skating. But she was afraid. Was her fear due to the fact that skating would be dangerous? Or was it holding her back from doing something that she might succeed at and enjoy? Grace wasn't sure.

One thing she knew was that using inline skates would be more difficult for her than it was for her friends. She decided to talk with her PT about it. He was glad she talked to him first and didn't just try it. He warned Grace that she could be seriously hurt if she tried inline skating now and fell. However, he showed her some new ways to work on her balance issues. He said that one day she might be able to inline skate—or use special skates so she wouldn't fall as easily. Grace was glad to have something to work toward.

Fears that can hold you back include:

- fear that you will try something and fail (so you don't even try)

- fear that you're not good enough or you don't measure up (so you end up with a lack of confidence or you set unrealistic goals to prove your worth)

- fear that others will judge you or make fun of you (so you avoid attention)

T.J., who was in seventh grade, had visible facial tics and stuttered sometimes. When his parents came in for a conference with his math teacher, Mr. Rodsky told them that T.J. had been asking for eighth-grade math. He had been working hard to complete the work, and Mr. Rodsky tried to support him in his goal. For a while it was going well. "However," Mr. Rodsky said, "T.J. came

to me in tears last week because he didn't understand his worksheet. He was very upset."

T.J.'s parents talked with their son. He said he was afraid that everyone thought he was dumb because of his tics and stuttering. He was pushing himself hard to show everyone how smart he was in math, but it was getting too hard for him.

Can you identify your fears? Can you tell if they are helping you or holding you back? Write down your answers or voice record them so you can refer back to them later in this chapter. Your support team may be able to help you figure out when something you're afraid of really is dangerous—and when your greatest danger may be your lack of confidence.

You might find it helpful to talk about your fears. Just like talking about your unpleasant feelings, talking about your fears can help you feel better. If you pick the right people to share your fears with, you may find that they truly understand and can be supportive. They may even be able to help you fight your fears.

EVA Eva had severe food allergies, severe asthma, and eczema. When she was in fifth grade, she began to worry that she would never be able to do things that she felt "normal kids" got to do. She worried about whether she would ever be able to move out of her dad's home. She worried that she'd never find a boy who liked her. She thought that talking to someone might help her feel better. But who?

Eva decided that talking to her two closest friends wasn't a good choice because neither of them had the same problems. And even though she liked them, she thought they might share her fears with other kids at school. She didn't like the idea of kids at school gossiping about her. Finally Eva decided to talk with her dad and her pulmonologist about her fears because they had always been so caring and helpful. She trusted them.

After Eva talked with her dad and doctor, she felt less alone. They understood her concerns and gave her great tips on how she could work to be independent and even date later in her life. Eva felt more optimistic about her future and more connected to her dad and doctor.

Two years later, Eva was talking with a friend who did not have a physical disability. Her friend shared similar fears about boys and growing up. Eva was surprised to find that someone without a physical issue worried about the same things as her. And she felt proud when she was able to understand and support her friend.

⟩⟩⟩⟩⟩ Common Fears

There are no right or wrong fears. But some fears are more common for kids and teens with physical challenges and disabilities. You may be surprised to learn that others have similar concerns to you. Here are a few of the more common fears and some advice for dealing with them.

I'm afraid kids will never see me as a regular kid. Nobody wants to be defined by his or her disability. One way to deal with this fear is to think of yourself as more than your disability. Look again at Chapter 1 for help on that. Next, be sure to share that real self—the "regular kid" personality that's inside you. That's what Chapter 2 is all about.

Making eye contact, starting conversations, showing an interest in others, and talking about your hobbies are all ways to communicate parts of who you are. You can practice by looking in the mirror and doing something important: Smiling! A smile lets others know that you are open to getting to know them.

I worry that I'll never be able to live without my parents. If you have a physical disability or challenge, you may have needs that someone has to help you with. It might seem like your mom or dad will always have to take care of those needs.

The good news is that there are lots of special tools and programs to help kids and grown-ups who have problems managing on their own. You can start asking your support team right away about some of these tools and programs that might be available to you. Also, your own skills may improve. Sometimes it just takes planning, hard work, and creativity to find a way to work around problems.

I worry that my disability will get worse. There are many types of physical difficulties, and many of them don't get worse. With many, you can work to improve your condition.

If you worry about getting worse, try talking to others instead of keeping your fears to yourself. First, figure out exactly what worries you. That way you can talk about it clearly and in detail. Then decide who to talk with. You might start with a parent, if that makes you feel most comfortable. But you will probably eventually need to talk with one of the professionals on your support team who is knowledgeable about your disability and can give you the answers you seek.

I worry I will never have a boyfriend or girlfriend. This is a worry that a lot of kids have as they approach their teen years. Dating—and even finding the right person to marry—can create anxiety for kids with or without physical difficulties.

Whether you're ready to date now or just worrying about the future, the best thing you can do is share with others who you are inside. If you can do that, you improve your chances of meeting people who might be interested in you. Even if you're not ready to date yet, it feels good to make connections with other people.

Some kids are nervous about dating someone with a physical difficulty or disability. They may think you're fragile or unable to be independent in particular settings. They may be trying to protect you by *not* starting a special relationship with you. Let people know that you're able to enjoy many of the same things they do. Show others what you're capable of, and talk to them about what you've done already.

You Can Say

- "Last weekend, I went fishing with my cousin at the creek. I love fishing!"

- "I've been working on some clay pots with handles. It's really hard, but I'm pretty good at ceramics."

- "I've been working on dribbling—do you like basketball, too?"

You can also talk about what you want to try to do.

I'm afraid I'll never be able to get a job. No matter how physically challenged you are, if you're able to read or listen to this book, you have the ability to think and plan.

So, while you may not be able to do some jobs that require certain physical skills, there are lots of different jobs you probably *can* do when you're older. You just have to find one that you have the right skills for and will enjoy. In high school, your guidance counselor may be able to guide you to find the right career or job. Your support team can help you, too. You don't have to do this job search on your own.

No one is able to do every job. Some people can't handle looking at blood, so they don't go into healthcare. If your physical issues rule out certain jobs, you're just like everyone else in being limited. As you get older, your support team can help you figure out what jobs you can do. If you build on your interests and strengths, you're likely to find a job that uses your skills and makes you happy.

Certain medical or physical conditions prevent adults from working on a regular basis. For these people, the government has special programs to help out. Sometimes the programs support people with money or special housing. If you qualify, you can get help connecting with these programs when the time is right. In the meantime, build up your abilities so your disabilities don't block you from jobs you might enjoy and do well.

Check out Chapter 6 for additional information about becoming more independent.

>>>>>> When Adults Try to Distract You from Negative Feelings

Imagine working up the courage to tell your mom that you're really nervous about whether your juvenile rheumatoid arthritis will get worse. You tell her you're very worried about your future and whether you'll be able to do the same things you can do today. Now imagine your mom responding something like this: "Don't worry about the future. You'll be fine."

How would you feel? Why would a parent say this?

The adults on your support team are working hard to help you make progress toward your goals. They might think that fears, sadness, or other negative feelings could prevent you from being motivated. They might believe you can move forward faster if you don't focus on your negative feelings. So they might try to minimize them or act like your fears aren't a big deal.

Another reason adults might minimize your fears is if they don't know whether your fears are realistic. Or maybe they don't know what you can do about them. Sometimes there is no easy answer or no way to know what will happen, so parents may try to help you focus on what you can control— things like doing your exercises.

> "My mom didn't understand why I wanted to talk about the future so much. I think it was uncomfortable for her, and she kept changing the subject. I finally told her I just wanted to know that she would help me through whatever happens. Eventually we had a good talk. I still worry a lot, but I feel like Mom and I will find a way to deal with things."—Tony, age 13

If adults try to distract you from your fears or other negative feelings, but you really just want to talk, you can teach them what you need from them. You might politely let them know that you don't need all the answers right away. You just need them to support you by listening.

You Can Say

- "I don't need you to tell me that everything is going to be fine. I just need someone to listen right now."

Being heard can be helpful, even when there is no quick solution to your worries.

>>>>>> Getting Professional Help

Some kids still have trouble smiling even after speaking with adults. If you still feel down or upset after talking with your support team, you may want to ask about getting help from a psychologist, psychiatrist, or social worker. These professionals are experts at helping children cope with tough times. (Read more about them on page 51.) Some of them even specialize in working with kids challenged by physical problems.

"Dr. Rubin helped me feel less hopeless and helpless in my life. I call him my feelings doctor."
—Sophie, age 13

Psychologists, psychiatrists, and social workers are trained to help kids (and adults) with their feelings. They can teach you strategies for dealing with tough times and getting through the stress. They can help you take back some power in your life. It's their job to help people problem-solve difficult or upsetting situations. They listen without judging you. They can help you decide what you need to accept and what you can work to change. And they can help you learn to be okay being you. All this help is called counseling.

Wouldn't it be great to learn from someone who specializes in understanding the needs of kids like you?

Some kids worry about going to counseling. They worry that others may see this as a sign of weakness. In reality, seeking help can be a sign of courage and strength. It shows that you want to work through obstacles and find healthy ways to cope.

If you think you might want to talk with one of these professionals about your feelings, ask your parents about it. You can also check in with other members of your support team. They may already know of a good professional who works with kids. Or they can help you find one. You may be able to find free or low-cost counseling in your area. Your parents or support team members may be able to research this possibility.

⟩⟩⟩⟩⟩ Five Other Ways to Get (and Stay!) Positive

Here are a few other things you can do to feel better when you just can't seem to smile.

1. Pump up your endorphins. Have you ever heard someone talk about a "runner's high"? When people exercise for a while, the brain releases chemicals called *endorphins* that make them feel good. Just as the body sends pain messages when you get hurt, it sends good feeling messages when you exercise a lot.

ANDRÉ

André, age 10, loved the idea of getting a natural "high" with endorphins and brought it up with his PT and OT. He said, "My doctor told me that endorphins are a great way to feel good. That got my attention!" Because he had muscular dystrophy, André had trouble walking and couldn't run.

André, the PT, and the OT came up with a plan for him to exercise even though he couldn't run. André would use his arms to pedal a desk bike, and he could dance for a while to his grandfather's old disco music. After doing the exercises for a week, André checked in with his doctor again. He said, "It was better than eating my favorite ice cream. It just makes me happy and calm inside."

Exercising is a great way to get endorphins pumping and feel good. It can take a little time to get over the hard part, though. Exercise doesn't always feel good at first. But if you stick with it for a while, it can be worth it!

- If you can run, run!
- If you can walk, walk a distance.
- If you can't walk, can you pedal a stationary bike for a while?
- If you can't use your legs, can you arm pedal on a desk bike?
- If you can't use your arms or legs, can you sway your head to music?
- Think about what makes you feel good in your body and, if it's safe, try it!

Exercising is not the only way to get those endorphins going. Laughing is also a great way. If you can have a nice, hearty laugh, you are almost certain to feel a rush of good feelings. Try telling jokes with friends or watching a funny movie or YouTube video. Or make up a silly story and act it out—you could even record your own video.

2. Join a peer support group. In many communities, groups of kids get together with an adult group leader to talk about things that bother them. For example, there may be a group made up of kids around your age who are living with the same physical disability as you. They may *really* understand what you go through each day, because they have similar struggles. In these peer support groups, you may learn some great strategies for dealing with tough situations.

"In my group I met this girl who also had problems moving her legs and arms well. She was so smart and was able to laugh at some of the mistakes she made. She also told me about how she managed some things at home, like getting dressed in the morning. I tried her ideas and they helped me."
—Margaret, age 10

You may find that a support group can help you feel connected, understood, and similar to others. The professionals on your support team may know if any local group would be a good fit for you.

3. Reflect on goals you've reached. You may sometimes feel frustrated when you don't reach one of your goals quickly. When you feel that way, it's helpful to remind yourself of your past successes.

Remembering goals that you worked hard at and reached can help you keep up the hope and motivation to reach new goals. Why not make a list of some obstacles that you overcame in the past? Post the list somewhere in your room or home where you can see it often and be reminded of your successes. You could even post a picture of yourself as you reached your goal (such as dribbling a basketball).

4. If a fear is holding you back, try to overcome it. For example, if you're afraid you won't do well in a spelling bee, spend more time practicing spelling so you do better. If you're afraid you'll never make friends, talk with an adult who can help you build up your social skills. If you're afraid you'll hurt yourself if you go snowboarding, talk with your PT about it. Maybe there are accommodations to help you do it safely, or maybe you can work on certain exercises to build up the strength to do it later. You will never know unless you ask!

5. Have fun to boost spirits. It's extremely important for all kids and adults to find activities they enjoy and people they like being around. Every day should include some fun time.

What activities give you pleasure? What people and things make you happy and make you smile? Make a point of doing those activities—or spending time with those people—as often as you can.

Try This

Here are a few things that have helped other kids enjoy time each day.

- hanging out with friends
- hanging out with family
- using the computer to see and speak with relatives who live far away
- drawing
- writing stories
- making comics
- baking
- making pizza
- playing board games
- playing video games
- making videos

It's important to remember that everyone feels upset, sad, frustrated, afraid, or angry at times. But you don't have to stay upset. Doing activities you love and spending time with loved ones are great ways to avoid getting stuck in negative feelings for a long time. All the ideas in this chapter are ways you can take control of your emotions and get back to feeling positive.

Chapter 6

Becoming More Independent

Most kids seek to have more control, choices, and responsibility as they get older. Maybe you want to go to the movies without a parent. Maybe you want to take charge of completing schoolwork without an adult telling you what to do and tracking your progress. Maybe you want a later bedtime or more freedom after school to hang out with friends. As you get even older, you might want to have a later curfew or earn money to buy things you like.

Do you ever wonder whether your physical challenges might keep you from being independent? While there may be some things you can't do on your own, many other things may be within your reach. For instance, can you help grocery shop and make and pack your lunches for school? Perhaps you can volunteer at a local animal shelter. You can find many creative ways to feel and be more independent.

RAMON

Ramon had cerebral palsy. He loved learning about marine life, and he also loved watching sports like soccer and basketball. But he didn't play any sports. Ramon watched his older sister's basketball games and wished he could play, too. But he felt "like a total spaz" and spent a lot of time focused on that. "My legs and body don't go in the same direction sometimes," he told his sister. "I can't even talk good. You guys understand what I say, but most people who meet me just smile and pretend to understand."

Ramon felt totally dependent upon his parents to speak up for him and to take care of his needs. One day when he was 10, Ramon realized that even his little brother was able to do more things than he could. His brother could play volleyball, talk with new kids, and make friends easily. Ramon talked with his mom and speech therapist about his anger and sadness over being "different."

Instead of getting a hug, Ramon got a homework assignment. He had to type out what he knew about his favorite topic—fish. Later, his special education teacher helped him put his knowledge into a PowerPoint presentation. It included images of different kinds of fish and other ocean creatures. Ramon then went to different classes and taught about this topic.

Later, he told his sister, "Even when kids didn't totally understand what I said, the PowerPoint showed the words that I was saying. Kids seemed a little surprised that I was smart. I was a little surprised, too! I didn't need Mom or Dad to help me do the research or writing. And nobody helped me give the presentation. Now I know I can find ways to feel independent. It's not always easy, but it's worth working at!"

Independence is a natural goal. It's important to strive for. Having more independence can lead you to feel more mature and responsible. You may feel more confident facing new challenges when you know you've already handled others. This chapter has lots of ways to help you increase your independence.

What Does It Mean to Be Independent?

You don't have to be living away from family and earning enough money to pay your own bills to be "independent." You don't even have to solve all your problems by yourself.

Independence means being able to think through situations you are faced with. It means setting goals and figuring out how to achieve those goals by being responsible and resilient. (If you're *resilient*, you're able to overcome setbacks and bounce back when things go wrong.) If you gave yourself some goals in Chapter 4, look at your list again (page 66). Do you have a plan for reaching them? Do you keep trying, even when it's hard? Being independent means you figure out how to reach realistic goals.

Part of independence is doing things on your own, but that's not the whole story. For example, imagine a grown man who gets dressed, brushes his teeth, cooks breakfast, drives his car, and goes to work. He does his job well, drives home, and does all his other chores and responsibilities. Is he independent? Maybe. What if he had someone reminding him to do each step? Imagine if his sister kept calling him to say, "Now it's time to brush your teeth" and "Now it's time to take out the garbage." Would you still think he's independent? Probably not.

So independence is partly about what you do. But it's also about how responsible you are and how good you are at problem solving. When you do what is expected of you without being asked, you are being independent. As you learn more about how to take care of yourself, you are becoming more independent.

Brad got bad burns on his face when he was little and still needed to put medication on his face every night. At the age of 11, he told his parents that he wanted to take responsibility for doing this. They doubted that he would remember to use the medication each night, but Brad happily proved them wrong. He set his watch to vibrate every night as a reminder. When the alarm went off, he stopped whatever he was doing at that time and put on the medication. He felt proud of himself and more independent from his parents.

An important part of being independent is knowing when to rely only on yourself and when to get help. For instance, unless your mom is an electrician, she would probably get help if she needed electrical work done in your home. A mature, independent parent knows who to call for help—and when to call them. Even professional athletes, who are among the world's best at what they do, get help from a support team. They may have coaches, teammates, and medical staff to help them if they are injured—maybe even a sports psychologist.

"I used to get so frustrated because I needed help getting from my wheelchair into bed. But I talked with my PT and got help building my upper body strength. She also helped me practice the movements I needed to make the transfer. Now I can do it alone, and it feels great! I'm so glad I got help from my PT."
—Jeremy, age 12

Independence can lead to a feeling of freedom, even when you get help from others.

Even though you might gradually gain more independence as you get older, you are already independent in some ways—maybe many! What are some things you do on your own or that you take responsibility for? Make a list of things you do that make you proud. Ask a parent for ideas if you need help.

Try This

Think of some positive things you do for yourself or others. Here are some examples. Maybe some of them will help you think of other ideas.

- Do you take care of some of your schoolwork on your own?

- Do you think of creative ideas for how your class can raise money for art supplies, a field trip, or something else?

- Do you find ways to cheer up your friends?

- Do you read a lot?

- Do you complete your chores without a parent reminding you?

- Do you take care of a pet?

- Do you help people at school or at home with the computer?

Focus on things you do that make you independent and happy. Remind yourself of them when you feel discouraged with not being able to do other things on your own.

People are independent when:

- They feel comfortable setting realistic goals.
- They figure out what they need to reach their goals.
- They keep working toward goals, even when it's tough.
- They are responsible at completing chores or tasks without reminders.

- They learn who to ask for help—and they ask when they need to.

- They are not afraid to think of new ideas and try new, safe experiences.

Show adults that you are ready for independence. If you want your parents or other adults to listen when you ask for more independence, show them that you deserve it! For example, imagine you want to have a job at home to earn money, but you never complete the chores you already have. Your parents probably won't think you're responsible enough to take on extra work. What if you ask for an alarm clock so you can wake up on your own each morning for school, but then always forget to set the clock? Your parents will learn that you still need them to take care of waking you up.

But what if you take care of your current responsibilities and follow through on any new ones you ask for? Then you're showing adults that you can handle more independence. Setting realistic goals and coming up with plans for reaching your goals also teaches adults that you're thinking in a mature way. These are good ways to earn more independence.

⟫⟫⟫⟫⟫ How Do You Try to Get What You Need?

Part of being independent is knowing what you need and trying to get it. Often this involves asking other people—other kids or important adults. To be successful at this, you will want to be respectful and clear.

You may have seen kids, or even adults, who boss people around. How would you feel about getting what you want that way? You probably know that being pushy or mean is not a way to have good relationships. That's called being *aggressive*. On the other hand, if you sit back and wait for others to guess what you need, you probably won't have much luck. If you do that, you're being too *passive*.

So what's the best way to let others know what you want or need? **By being assertive!** When you are assertive, you speak up when you need support or you want something. You respectfully share your opinions with others. You don't try to force others to follow your rules, and you don't insult people you don't agree with. You are clear, direct, and respectful.

JACK

Thirteen-year-old **Jack** loved music and wanted to join his friends' band, but he wasn't sure how to ask if they would let him in. He just hung out with them at school and sometimes when they practiced. He complimented them on their sound. They knew he played guitar, so he hoped they would eventually invite him to play with them. But after waiting and hoping for a while, he figured he needed a new strategy.

At first, Jack was really mad that they didn't invite him to play. He thought about yelling at the band members and letting them know how they weren't very good friends. He thought he might threaten not to be their friend anymore if they didn't let him in the band. But he knew that wasn't a great approach. He didn't like the idea of being mean. And he didn't want to be in the band if they didn't really want him.

Finally, Jack spoke up. He said, "I've been practicing my electric guitar a lot. I like the kind of music you guys play, and I think I could add to your sound. I would love to be a part of your group. Can I play with you sometime and show you?"

Jack's first strategy was passive: He just sat back and waited for his friends to invite him to play. It didn't work, probably because nobody knew what he wanted. He came up with a second idea that was aggressive: He could yell at them and threaten them. He wisely chose not to do that, though. It didn't feel right to him, and he knew he wouldn't be happy getting in the band that way.

Finally, he chose an assertive approach: He respectfully asked them if he could play. Here's what happened.

JACK

Jack's friends were glad he spoke up. But they told him they didn't need another guitar player right then. Good news, though. They invited him to come to practice more often. A couple of times when the guitarist couldn't make it, Jack played with them. They started calling Jack their backup guitarist. That was enough for Jack for now. He felt like he was finally part of a group and doing something that felt "normal."

Whether a person has physical problems or not, the assertive path is most often the one that works best. Being aggressive, such as by yelling, threatening, or scaring someone, can cause hurt feelings and other problems. It can lead to loss of pride and confidence, too. Being passive, and just hoping that someone will know what you need, can often be disappointing. Even if you feel that others *should* know what you need, they may not. Speaking up, sharing your thoughts, and being respectful often lead to more positive reactions.

You Can Say

- "Excuse me, Mrs. Kelley, but I'm having trouble with this math problem. Could you help me?"

- "Hey, Dad, could we talk? I was wondering if I could have a raise in allowance."

- "Hi, Anna. I heard you guys are going to the yogurt shop after school. Would it be okay if I come, too?"

However, being assertive does not mean being impatient or demanding. For example, when you want to ask your gym teacher for help with something, but he's busy helping another student, it's important to wait. This might look like you are being passive, but really you're being polite and patient. Being polite not only helps you get along better with others. It can help you get what you need, too. People are more likely to want to help you if you treat them well.

Are you assertive? Think about how you act most of the time. Does your style work for you? Here are some things to think about.

- **Do other people feel respected by how you speak with them?** If you're not sure, ask them. For example, "How did you feel hearing what I said to you?" If people say you are loud, mean, pushy, bossy, or bullying, you're probably acting too aggressively.

- **Do other people know what you need?** Think about whether you usually get what you need or whether you feel understood. If you don't, maybe you are being too passive. If you're not sure, you can ask: "I just want to check that I communicated the right things. What do you think I need or want right now?"

- **Do you pick the right time to share your thoughts?** If someone has the time to listen, it's probably the right time! If you don't always get a good response, consider whether your timing could be better. Speak up for yourself when people aren't busy with other things or other people.

- **Do you know who you need to speak up to for help?** Think about the list of go-to people you brainstormed on page 90.

- **Do other kids get listened to more than you?** If the answer is yes, watch what they do. Can you pick out how they get the attention they need and if they clearly state their needs?

>>>>> Parents and Independence

The role of parents is to keep you safe and to prepare you for your future. Safety is usually the top priority of parents. Remember, they once saw you as a tiny infant. They took care of you and all of your needs. They may still have to take care of some of your needs. But they may not be sure when to pull back and let you be more independent. They may want to protect you and reduce the stress in your life, so they take care of some needs that you could now do on your own.

"My mom always babies me. She won't let me do anything. She keeps saying I'm going to get hurt or fall. It's so annoying!"
—Kristen, age 11

If Kristen's experience matches your own, and you also want more independence, it might be time to teach your parents. Yes, you do have that power! If you yell "Back off!" at your mom or dad, they probably won't hear the real message. On the other hand, if you calmly explain what you would like to try on your own, they can give you their feedback. Maybe they will agree.

Be specific when you talk with your parents. Tell them exactly what you want to do and why you think you can handle it. Be ready to give the reasons you think you can do these new things. Maybe you have gained new abilities or matured as a person. For example, have you shown more responsibility lately around the house or at school? Have you made progress in your therapy? Have you accomplished things that are similar to the new one you want to try?

When you talk to your parents, keep an open mind. If they say no to your ideas, try to understand their point of view. Is what you want to do dangerous? Will they worry about your safety or your feelings? Could your goals for independence in certain areas set back your therapy progress? If you don't agree with their reasons, try not to get too upset. Agree to think about their comments, and maybe you can explain your disagreement later.

Try This

When you talk with your parents, keep the following tips in mind. If you are respectful and prepared, you have a better chance of being heard and getting the changes you want.

1. **Be specific.** Have a specific goal and specific reasons why you think you should be able to do it.

2. **Be realistic.** Don't ask to do something that your parent will think is very risky or hard.

3. **Get help.** Before talking to your parent, consider speaking with someone from your support team about what you might try more independently that won't set back your health or progress.

4. **Set the tone.** Don't talk when you are very emotional or when your parents are busy. Make sure you all have the time for this important talk. You can even schedule it ahead of time.

5. **Show appreciation.** It's always helpful to start off any meeting thanking your family members for what they have done.

6. **Listen.** After you explain what you want, listen to what your parent says with an open mind.

With these six steps, you may be able to teach your parents and others an important lesson about you. You are letting them know that you are able to communicate calmly and clearly. You can be realistic and appreciative, and you can listen to the opinions of others. In other words, you are teaching grown-ups that you are growing up, too.

You can put as much work into increasing your independence as you are ready for. Whether you're trying to get more control at home, in class, with your support team, or in your social world, remember that hard work often pays off. That doesn't mean that you'll always get over every obstacle or problem. It doesn't mean you can make yourself walk if you're in a wheelchair. But it means you can move forward in some areas faster if you work hard.

Some days you may feel lazy or bored with the exercises. You may even feel angry that you have to do the work on your area of physical disability. You could give up, right?

Wrong!

Giving up means not taking control. Everyone has days when they need a quick vacation or break. That's okay. Talk with your parents, teachers, and therapists about how often you feel like you need a day off to keep up your motivation. And then get back on track and keep working toward your goal of independence.

Chapter 7

Getting the Most Out of School (And Thinking About Your Future)

Sometimes the challenges that we all face in the present can keep us from looking toward the future. You may feel like you have enough to worry about just getting through today! Pressures at school, at home, and with friends—these give you plenty to focus on. Your physical difficulties add even more responsibilities and challenges. Who has time to think about the future?

But thinking about the possibilities that await you and the adventures you might have can be lots of fun. Not only that, it can also be really good for you. Having goals for the future keeps you focused, motivated, and positive. Having hopes and dreams feels good.

>>>>>> Planning for School

For most kids your age, the immediate future involves more school. But first, let's look to the *past*. We're talking about a law called the Education of All Handicapped Children Act, which was enacted in 1975. This law has been updated over time and is now often referred to as the Individuals with Disabilities Education Act, or IDEA. But its goal remains the same. It helps kids with physical, learning, or other disabilities get a good education despite their challenges.

Because of this law, you may have another support team besides the one you learned about in Chapter 3. This is a group of people who help plan your schooling to make sure you get the education you need and deserve.

You might have a Committee on Special Education, or CSE, if you're receiving special education. Or you might have a 504 Committee. Either way, these people work to make sure you receive an appropriate education. Your committee likely includes your parents, your teacher or teachers, and some of your support team (for example, your PT). It also might have other professionals who know how to support kids with physical or other challenges in school.

The committee usually meets once each year to make recommendations for your next grade. But it might meet more often if adjustments need to be made to your support plan. The members review how things went the previous year and whether you met your goals. They discuss your abilities and strengths as well as the areas that continue to be a challenge for you. They brainstorm ways to support you in the upcoming year.

THOMAS

Thomas was a bright 10-year-old boy who was legally blind. He was able to see shadows, so he could walk around with the aid of a blind sensing stick. Thomas loved school, but he might not have been as successful without the support set up by his CSE. Here are some of the key supports they set up for him:

- audiobooks so he could listen to the book that his classmates read
- meetings with a vision therapist who was teaching him to read braille
- books in braille so he could build up his reading skills
- a voice recognition program on his school computer that typed the words he spoke
- a computer with braille on the keyboard
- taking tests in a separate room where someone read the questions to him and wrote down the answers he gave
- meetings with a special instructor to help him safely get around the school
- permission to leave class early with a friend to get to his next classroom before all the kids were in the hallway

Thomas also spent some time each day in the resource room. There, he got the support of a special education teacher. She knew how to help him learn in a way that fit his learning style and needs. Thomas went to the resource room to get help learning math concepts and organizing long essays.

None of these supports gave Thomas answers to tests or an easy ride through school. He still had to learn the schoolwork and learn to be independent. The supports gave him the same chance other kids had to do well in school. Thomas was proud that he was able to perform well at school. He told his father, "No one would even know that I'm blind if they just looked at my report card or asked what I learned in school today."

Like Thomas, you might have a CSE or 504 Committee, but you may not have met the members. If you're not sure, ask your parents if you have one of these committees and, if so, who is on it. You can also ask what they discuss and when they meet. Your mom or dad may have gone to CSE meetings to plan for your needs. If you're interested, you might be able to attend your committee's meeting, too.

Your CSE writes all your supports or special interventions into a legal document called an Individualized Educational Program, also known as an Individualized Education Plan or **IEP.** This plan is a promise from the school to you that they will help you in ways that they believe are right. For example, all the supports Thomas got (page 127) were written into his IEP.

Have you ever been to a CSE or 504 meeting? This meeting may be called an IEP meeting. Some kids attend their CSE or 504 meetings and some don't. If you don't attend right now, this is absolutely fine. If there are things you need but don't have, you can tell members of your support team who attend the meeting. Over time, though, you might want to work to be more involved in the planning meetings where your goals for the upcoming year are decided.

Think about how it might feel if you do attend the meeting. You would get to listen to the professionals talk about how they want to help you. You could share your thoughts about your strengths and needs. It might be a cool experience! You might feel like you're taking more control over your education. That always feels good.

> "When I was younger, I didn't want to go to a meeting with adults. Now that I'm a little older, I decided to see what it was like. I went to my first CSE meeting last week. I'm glad I did. I got to share some of my own goals and they put some of them into my school plan!"—Eli, age 12

If you want to go to the meeting, ask a parent if it's okay. Sometimes the team needs to make some adult decisions, and it could confuse or overwhelm you. You might just come for part of the meeting.

Try This

If you go to your CSE or 504 meeting, spend some time thinking about these questions. They will help you prepare beforehand and get the most out of the meeting when you're there.

- There may be several people you don't know there. Say hello to everyone and ask for everyone's name before the meeting begins.

- The team is there to talk about you. That can feel uncomfortable for some kids, so think about whether you're up for that. Remember, everyone who attends is there to help you.

- Also remember that everyone there has lots of experience and knows how to help kids with physical or other difficulties.

- They might ask you to talk about your physical challenges. Plan ahead so you know what you want to tell them.

- You can ask them to explain anything you don't understand.

- You can ask them what help they decided to give you.

- You can ask them for different or more help, but you will need to explain why.

- If the team does not give you everything you want, stay cool, and talk with your support team later.

⟩⟩⟩⟩⟩⟩ Testing for a Better Future

Your support team and your CSE or 504 Committee need to have up-to-date information about what you need help with. Testing is one way to check on how you have changed over time. You don't want a team to make recommendations for you based on old information. So, if you feel annoyed or anxious about taking tests, remember that they help your committee make the best decisions for you. They need to know where your strengths are and what goals you might still need to work on.

Hailey, age 9, started crying at home. She was upset that she had to go through a bunch of testing at school before her CSE meeting. She yelled at her mother: "I hate that stupid testing. Are they trying to figure out if I'm dumb or something? Maybe they're trying to see if I'm ever going to be able to get better. It makes me so nervous!"

After Hailey's mom helped her calm down, they talked. Her mom told her that her IEP listed a lot of physical therapy goals. The testing would show if she still needed to work on them or if she needed different goals. For example, she would be asked to stand for 15 seconds to see whether she could reach that goal now. In addition, she would be tested on whether she could use her arms to catch a ball that is gently tossed to her. She couldn't fail any of these tests, and she wouldn't get graded on them.

Hailey went through the testing and was pleased to learn that she could stop doing one of the PT exercises because her range of motion had improved so much. She was given new exercises to help her get even stronger. Hailey found the results of her tests to be interesting.

Have you ever been asked to take tests by your committee? If so, how did you feel? Do you feel more like Hailey at the beginning of her story or more like her at the end?

There are a lot of tests that your committee might want you to take, especially if you have an IEP. The main goal of testing is not to upset or punish you. It's to help get the right plan for you in school so that you can be successful.

Here are a few of the tests or assessments. (You may take some, all, or none of them.)

- **Psychological testing** helps determine how you learn best so your teachers can teach you in the most effective ways. These tests also look at how you feel about yourself to see if you might benefit from counseling (see pages 102–103).

- **Educational testing** looks at whether you have strong school talents. It checks what subjects are easy for you and if you need help in a subject or learning area.

- **Speech-language testing** looks at how you speak and understand language to see if you would benefit from help in those areas.

- **Physical therapy testing** helps determine your progress and challenges with regard to your physical abilities.

- **Occupational therapy testing** looks at the smaller movements of your body and movements and skills you need every day for writing and reading, for example.

One surprise you might find is that the testing can be fun. For example, the psychological testing gives you a chance to play with blocks (yes—even at your age)! You may enjoy learning which tasks are easy for you, which are so-so, and which are challenging. You may also realize that some skills that were challenging in the past are not as difficult now.

When you take a test, your therapist is learning more about how to help you. Testing is not only about checking your areas of weakness or disability. Your therapists are also checking up on their treatment plan. Are they doing a good job of giving you the right exercises? Are they seeing you often enough? Do they need to rethink their plan for you? **You might be even stronger than they realized!**

LIAM

Liam was upset that his mother had to lift him out of bed each morning to put him into his wheelchair. When he was 10, he went through testing that showed that his arms were really strong. His PT got him a bar that hung over his bed. Liam was excited to learn the movements he needed to lift himself into a sitting position and then into his wheelchair. Without testing, he hadn't known just how strong his upper arms were.

Testing opened the door for Liam to focus on new activities for the upcoming year. He looked at his future in a new, more optimistic way.

Testing can help you think about future jobs, too. Some kids with physical challenges worry about whether they can ever get a job when they grow up. *Vocational testing* can help you figure out which jobs you might enjoy and which jobs are a good fit with your skills. The word vocation basically means **job.** When you get into high school, you may get the chance to do some vocational testing to figure out what jobs would be good for you.

Many professionals may not need to be able to walk to do their jobs, including psychologists, video editors, accountants, writers, and more. People who speak clearly can work to get a job on the radio. Today, many office jobs and sales jobs can be done from home or partly from home.

Vocational testing may check out your interests, strengths, and personal characteristics. For example, would you describe yourself as more shy or more outgoing?

Do you like to have a good set of directions to follow, or do you prefer to be more creative? After testing, the evaluator may be able to let you know if your learning style and interests match those of people in a certain career. You can learn about all sorts of vocational possibilities through vocational testing. There are many fun, unusual, and interesting ways to earn money when you grow up.

As you get older and closer to thinking about working, ask your support team if it's the right time to talk about getting vocational testing done.

>>>>> You and Your Future

As you learn more about yourself, you will slowly begin to find answers to important questions. You may start to think about whether you will go to college, go to a technical school that helps train you for a particular job, or start working immediately after you get out of high school. Your parents, support team, and even your CSE or 504 Committee can help you figure this out.

As you get older, you will also get a better idea of how to share your thoughts, feelings, and personality with others. You may expand your support team and find even more friends who are a good fit for you. We hope you will gain more and more confidence in the maturing you.

Enjoy each step as you travel through the journey of life. As you do, remember:

You are not your disability—it's just a small part of you.

Kids won't know who you are unless you show them.

It's normal to feel frustrated, but giving up is harder in the long run.

Your support team is there to—you guessed it—support you!

It's healthy to talk about your fears.

It's okay to share feelings of anger, sadness, or jealousy with your parents—they can only help if they know what you're feeling.

You can take some control of your future plans.

We have talked a lot about goals in this book, but here's one important last suggestion: **Make sure you spend some time using your areas of ability and doing things that you enjoy.** Life isn't always about working toward goals. Sometimes it's about laughs, fun, and being with people you love. Pride and happiness can come from working hard toward goals *and* working hard to appreciate the good times!

Note to Parents

When your child was first born, you probably realized that you would be starting a journey of discovery. You may have silently questioned who your child would become as a toddler, child, teen, and adult. Because your child has a physical disability or challenge, you might have had other questions, such as "How will this physical condition affect my son's life?" and "How can I enable my daughter to be independent and reach her potential?"

As the parent of a child with a physical difficulty or disability, it's important for you to communicate as openly as possible with your child, empower your child, and take care of yourself.

Communicating with Your Child

Communicating with a tween or young teen is sometimes a challenge. As children grow up, they often realize that parents don't always understand how they think and feel. You might try to start a conversation with your child about how she* feels about herself or her experiences. In this way, you highlight the fact that your child has independent perceptions and views.

---

*For ease of reading, we are alternating "she" and "he" in reference to your child, but the information applies to boys and girls alike.

If you want to talk, set aside some time so the conversation isn't rushed and your child knows that you are really interested. Let him know that you want to ask some questions about his thoughts and feelings. It can be useful to ask for permission to talk about certain topics. You don't want him to feel that this is a test or there is an obligation to answer all questions. If neither you nor your child feels pressured, the discussion can be interesting, insightful, and even fun.

Consider using the following list of questions to start the conversation. If you're willing, your child may appreciate you answering some questions as well.

- If you could pick an age to be at forever, what age would you pick? Why?

- Is your life more stressful now than in the past? If so, why?

- How would you describe your personality?

- What are your areas of talent?

- What makes you laugh?

- What makes you happy?

- What annoys you?

- What frustrates you?

- How do you feel about going to school each day?

- How do the kids treat you?

- How do your teachers treat you?

- On a scale of 1–10, how much do your physical problems affect you on a day-to-day basis? How much do you think your physical issues will affect your future?

- How would you describe what it's like for you to have your physical difficulties?

- What three things do you want me to know about you?

- What three things do you want other people to know about you?

- If you didn't have a physical issue, what would be most different about your daily life?

- What can I do to make the next few years go smoother for you?

- Are there things I do that embarrass you? If so, what are they?
- How do you usually feel?

If your child reports feeling burdened by or upset with her physical problem or medical illness, it's important to let her know that you are there to listen, help, and support her. It's okay to admit that you do not know exactly what it feels like to have her physical disability (or difference), but you are there for her nonetheless.

Initially, kids may not realize that they can feel pride in how they deal with their difficulty. They may focus on the negative or focus on tasks that are too challenging for them to achieve right now. You may want to point out the courage that they show and the respect you have for them as they struggle to overcome obstacles. You can be the mirror that reflects back some of the positive qualities and abilities you see in your child.

Empowering Your Child

Parents seek to protect their children from harm. When a child is physically fragile or vulnerable, parents sometimes go into super-guardian mode. This is a natural reaction but may have unwanted consequences, such as leading your child to believe he is helpless or unable to manage without you and postponing his ability to feel independent.

Of course you want to help your child avoid dangerous situations, and you don't want your child to feel overwhelmed or demoralized if a situation is too difficult to manage. However, at any age and with almost any disability, children can handle certain tasks and responsibilities independently or with minimal help or guidance. It is through these experiences of independence and accomplishment that children learn to feel pride and motivation to try new things.

For example, if a child is unable to walk, focus on what she can do. Does she like funny videos? Perhaps she can write a script, shoot scenes, and edit a short, funny movie. Think creatively, and come up with activities that your child can accomplish and enjoy.

If you find that your child is often focused on limitations rather than abilities, or your child frequently seems sad, depressed, anxious, or angry, it may be time to consider adding a mental health professional to the support team. Mental health professionals can help teach children how to face adversity, bounce back from disappointments, set goals, self-reflect, cope with emotional discomfort, problem-solve, and become advocates for themselves. Many mental health professionals are also available to guide parents on how to help their kids cope with difficult times.

Helping Yourself

Be kind to yourself. Turn to others for support when you feel stressed or overwhelmed. Talk with a spouse, parent, sibling, or friend. You may also be able to talk with someone on your child's support team for advice and guidance on how to continue protecting your child while also encouraging independence.

Make sure you have enjoyable grown-up time, too. Participate in activities you love, spend time with other adults, and find ways to relax and laugh. Taking care of yourself allows you to continue to have the emotional energy to be supportive to your child.

Raising a child with physical challenges is about raising a child first. Remind yourself to focus on your entire child and enjoy the giggles, fun times, and carefree moments. As you watch your children work on goals, have accomplishments, and mature, support them through the tough times but don't forget to celebrate the milestones and joyful times together, too.

Resources

Able to Play: Overcoming Physical Challenges by Glenn Stout. Houghton Mifflin, 2012. This book tells the stories of four big league baseball players who overcame physical challenges to excel at their sport.

A Bad Case of Stripes by David Shannon. Scholastic Inc., 1998. This book for younger readers illustrates how even though kids sometimes change who they are just to fit in, it's okay to think differently—or be different in some way.

Being Me: A Kid's Guide to Boosting Confidence and Self-Esteem by Wendy L. Moss. Magination Press, 2011. A book to help kids explore their strengths and be confident in school with friends and with themselves.

Disabilities: My Child's Special Needs
U.S. Department of Education
www2.ed.gov/parents/needs/speced/edpicks.jhtml
This page features resources for parents of children with special needs.

Juvenile Arthritis Association
juvenilearthritis.org
Resources for children and young adults diagnosed with juvenile arthritis.

KidsHealth
kidshealth.org
A general resource for parents, kids, and teens on various diseases, disabilities, and general health.

Learning to Feel Good and Stay Cool: Emotional Regulation Tools for Kids with AD/HD by Judith M. Glasser and Kathleen Nadeau. Magination Press, 2013. This book can be useful for kids with or without ADHD. It helps readers identify feelings and find ways to cope with them.

Muscular Dystrophy Association
mda.org
A healthcare resource for families with muscular dystrophy and other neuromuscular diseases.

Skyla: The One-Legged Seagull by Deborah Bowman. Boulden Publishing, 2008. A story about a seagull who only had one leg but learned to have confidence and try new experiences.

Stick Up for Yourself! Every Kid's Guide to Personal Power and Self-Esteem by Gershen Kaufman, Lev Raphael, and Pamela Espeland. Free Spirit Publishing, 1999. An excellent resource for kids on learning and building assertiveness skills.

United Cerebral Palsy
ucp.org
Provides support for people with a wide range of disabilities.

What to Do When You're Scared and Worried: A Guide for Kids by James J. Crist. Free Spirit Publishing, 2004. Advice, reassurance, and ideas for kids dealing with worries and fears, including help for hard-to-handle fears they can't manage on their own. Includes a section for adults.

Index

About the Authors

Wendy L. Moss, Ph.D., ABPP, FAASP, has over 30 years of experience working with children and families as a psychologist in schools, clinics, hospitals, and private practice settings. She earned her doctorate in clinical psychology, is a certified school psychologist, and has been appointed as a fellow in the American Academy of School Psychology. She has also been awarded the status of "Diplomate in School Psychology" by the American Board of Professional Psychology. Dr. Moss is the author of several books, including *Children Don't Come with an Instruction Manual: A Teacher's Guide to Problems That Affect Learners*; *Being Me: A Kid's Guide to Boosting Confidence and Self-Esteem*; and *Bounce Back: How to Be a Resilient Kid*. She is the coauthor of *School Made Easier: A Kid's Guide to Study Strategies and Anxiety-Busting Tools* (with Robin A. DeLuca-Acconi, LCSW) and *The Tween Book: A Growing-Up Guide to the Changing You* (with Donald A. Moses, M.D.).

Susan A. Taddonio, D.P.T., M.A., P.T., has more than 20 years of experience working with children and families as a physical therapist in schools, homes, and private practice. She is also an assistant professor at Touro College and a clinical instructor at Stonybrook University. Dr. Taddonio holds a doctorate in physical therapy from Stonybrook University in New York. She was inspired to go into the field of physical therapy by her uncle, who had polio. As a child, she saw him perform ordinary as well as extraordinary tasks—such as doing construction jobs—even when using crutches. She believed that his mental attitude helped him excel and be successful, and she hopes to help kids find that same positive attitude.

Other Great Books from Free Spirit

For ages 8–13.
128 pp.; paperback;
2-color; illust.; 6" x 9"

For ages 9–14.
192 pp.; paperback;
illust.; 7" x 9"

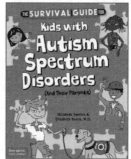

For ages 9–13.
240 pp.; paperback; full color;
illust.; 7" x 9"

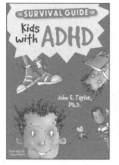

For ages 8–12.
128 pp.; paperback;
2-color; illust.; 6" x 9"

For ages 10 & under.
128 pp.; paperback;
2-color; illust.; 6" x 9"

For ages 10–14.
160 pp.; paperback;
2-color; illust.; 6" x 9"

For ages 8 & up.
112 pp.; paperback;
illust.; 6" x 9"

Find all the Free Spirit **SURVIVAL GUIDES** for Kids
at www.freespirit.com/survival-guides-for-kids

For pricing information, to place an order, or to request a free catalog, contact:

Free Spirit Publishing Inc.
217 Fifth Avenue North • Suite 200 • Minneapolis, MN 55401-1299 • toll-free 800.735.7323
local 612.338.2068 • fax 612.337.5050 • help4kids@freespirit.com • www.freespirit.com